RUN

Your Personal Guide
to Winning Public Office

RUN

Your Personal Guide
to Winning Public Office

Senator Marian Walsh

BOSTON | 2013

RUN: Your Personal Guide to Winning Public Office

GRAND COVE PUBLISHING LLC
www.marianwalsh.com

To reach the author or Grand Cove Publishing, email: marian@marianwalsh.com

ISBN: 978-0-9893440-0-5

Other available versions:

Digital Distribution
ISBN: 978-0-9893440-1-2

Manufactured in the United States of America
First Edition

Design by John Lotte for Blue Mountain Marketing

Cover design by Michael Gross for Blue Mountain Marketing
On the cover: "Freedom of Speech" by Norman Rockwell
Printed by permission of the Norman Rockwell Family Agency,
Copyright © 1943 The Norman Rockwell Family Entities

This book is dedicated to a great American patriot,

in loving gratitude, my husband,

Paul Vernon Buckley.

It is not the critic who counts, not the man who points out how the strong man stumbles or where the doer of deeds could have done better. The credit belongs to the man who is actually in the arena, whose face is marred by dust and sweat and blood, who strives valiantly, who errs and comes up short again and again, because there is no effort without error or shortcoming, but who knows the great enthusiasms, the great devotions, who spends himself for a worthy cause; who, at the best, knows, in the end, the triumph of high achievement, and who, at the worst, if he fails, at least he fails while daring greatly, so that his place shall never be with those cold and timid souls who knew neither victory nor defeat.

—THEODORE ROOSEVELT,
"CITIZENSHIP IN A REPUBLIC" SPEECH AT THE SORBONNE,
PARIS, APRIL 23, 1910

Contents

Introduction

On January 6, 1941, eleven months before the attack on Pearl Harbor and the United States' entry into WWII, President Franklin D. Roosevelt addressed Congress on the "Four Freedoms." His words brought to life the principles the nation's founders fought for, which the country was about to go to war in order to uphold—and that still live and thrive in her citizens.

Roosevelt's words inspired artist Norman Rockwell to artistically portray the "Four Freedoms." The paintings he created—one of which, titled "Freedom of Speech," is on the cover of this book—have since become iconic symbols of America's highest ideals.

"Freedom of Speech" captures the sacred space created when a citizen participates in political discourse honestly and directly. Whenever someone stands up at a town meeting, addresses fellow citizens or elected officials in a public forum, or declares himself or herself as a candidate for office, that freedom Rockwell so vividly described with his brush is reinvigorated and affirmed.

A print of this illustration, a gift from staff member Mary Ellen Rousell, hung in my State House office. It inspired, centered, and guided me as a citizen and as an elected official. It serves to express the power and dignity of each citizen's participation in our government.

The Three Levels of Government in America

Federal Government

The federal government makes and enforces laws affecting the entire nation. It maintains the military, sets foreign policy and regulates the national economy and foreign trade. It also prints money, provides Social Security and Medicare programs, and regulates national business and transportation.

The federal government manages our national court system.

State Government

The fifty state governments ensure public safety and provide public education and housing. The fifty states also share with the federal government authority to regulate banks, insurance, hospitals, health care, and licensing of the trades and professions.

Each state manages a court system.

Local Government

State law organizes local governments into cities, counties and towns.

Local government provides public safety (police and fire) roads, water, sewer, parks, public health, schools and libraries.

The Three Branches of the Federal Government

Legislative Branch	Executive Branch	Judicial Branch
The legislative branch is composed of lawmakers who are elected by the people. There are two branches of Congress: the House of Representatives, whose members serve two-year terms, and the Senate, whose members serve six-year terms. Each citizen has one Congressman and two U.S. Senators. They make national public policy, declare war, levy taxes, pass our national budget, and approve the Cabinet Secretaries and Supreme Court and judicial nominations of the president. The Senate ratifies treaties.	The executive branch is headed by our elected president, who serves a term of four years, and can be elected twice. The president manages the affairs of the nation. The president is also the Commander in Chief of the military, and the world ambassador for our country. Federal judges and major federal officials are appointed by the president, subject to Senate confirmation.	The judicial branch interprets the laws passed by the legislative branch, settles disputes, and applies the Constitution to protect citizens. State judges are appointed by the executive and/or legislative branches, or in some states are elected by the people. Each state determines its judicial appointment process. State judges settle disputes and apply their state constitution. Most states and the federal government require judges to be lawyers.

Foreword

Running for Office Starts at Home

This book is for candidates, and for those who aspire to be candidates. Whether you are running for office for the first time, running for reelection, or are simply thinking you might want to run someday in the future, the information set forth in the following pages will inspire, equip, and support you. The words written here are also for those who care about someone running for office, and who want to acquire knowledge to better support their candidacy in a meaningful, effective manner. Finally, what you are about to read will empower you as a voter who desires more authentic and relevant political conversations for candidates. If you love politics and are searching for the best way to get more involved in the political process—possibly by running for public office—this book will show you how to be the best candidate you can be, and how to win.

As a citizen, I know that America is Number One. I also know that we can continue to improve and become even better than we are today. By "Number One," I mean the greatest place for community, freedom, dignity, and shared responsibility. Number One for me is a country where each individual matters and everyone is welcome.

It is a place made greater by the expectations and commitment of its people and it depends on the self-government of those people to survive and thrive.

One way we fulfill these expectations and express our commitment is by participating in the political process. We make our voices heard every time we cast a vote. Being self-governed means it's up to us as individuals to ensure that our elected leadership truly reflects the needs and concerns of our communities and neighborhoods, and of our country as a whole. I wrote this book in the hope that more of us will get involved in governing, so more of our voices will be heard, and we will continue to realize more fully the potential of America.

We do this one step at a time, just like we do most important things. If you are a parent, think back to that moment when you brought your newborn son or daughter home from the hospital. Maybe you had help from family and friends, had a bookshelf full of parenting books and some parenting blogs bookmarked, or were surrounded by people who offered advice. The parents who came before you gave you a roadmap to follow but ultimately the decisions that would shape your child's future were yours alone.

That same idea applies to many of life's challenges. You've probably gone on a job interview, coached a Little League team, or sat on the board at your condominium association. You've volunteered your time, cared for an aging parent, or joined the PTA. You've brought your own knowledge, values, and heart to a job or cause that meant something to you personally. You took a risk, getting involved in something larger than yourself without knowing exactly what was in store. You trusted that you could figure it out and succeed.

Yet when you read the title of this book, you may have thought to yourself, "I could never run for office." Why not? Running for public office isn't all that different from being a parent, interviewing for a job, or, for that matter, getting up and going to work every day.

You might be surprised to learn that running for office isn't terribly hard. Your everyday experiences as a citizen, all of your various relationships and ordinary daily responsibilities, have already prepared you to run. You don't need any special, secret knowledge. You know enough and you have enough, right now.

Running for and holding public office requires little more than making informed decisions based on the facts, your values, and getting to know your fellow citizens. You'll need the courage to be yourself, and a desire to do the right thing. Chances are you're doing that already.

In fact, it's those real-life experiences and everyday qualities that qualify you to take leadership in your community. Who understands the people's concerns, dreams, headaches, and fears better than one of their own? And who better to bring those important issues to light and ignite change than someone who experiences them personally? In other words, who better than you?

I did not come from a political family. My father, Francis Xavier, was born in 1911, the son of an Irish immigrant mother and the youngest of nine. His mother—who, although well read and financially savvy, never went to school beyond the fourth grade—rented out rooms in her Dorchester, Massachusetts home to pay for his education. He became a doctor and served in an Army field hospital in the South Pacific during WWII.

Whenever I had what my father called a "face" on, a bad attitude, he would say, "Let me ask you a few questions. Do you have a roof over your head? Are you getting three square meals a day? Is anyone shooting at you? No? So what kind of day are you having?"

I grew up steeped in that profound sense of gratitude and got a firsthand view of the great things passion can achieve. My father cared deeply about public health and started one of the first well-baby clinics in Boston. He also worked with combat veterans suffering from what we now call post traumatic stress disorder, and helped start the initial programs serving that population at the Veterans' Administration hospital. My father combined a strong education with faith, and he believed in positive change. His model of knowledge tempered by conscience became my model as well.

When I decided to run for office, he was the first person I told. I called him collect from a pay phone at a White Hen Pantry convenience store in West Roxbury, and said, "I know what I really want to do. I want to run for state representative." There was a long pause. Then he told me to go home, lie down, and shut my mouth. I think he was afraid for me, afraid of what I was getting myself into.

Come morning, I still felt the same way and I decided to run. I'll write a lot more about my first campaign throughout this book, but the short story is this: An established incumbent held the state rep seat, then stepped down to seek another elected office. The field to replace him became crowded. There were six of us in the Democratic primary, some were experienced candidates. I won.

I became the first woman from the Suffolk and Norfolk district to serve in either the State Senate or House of Representatives in Massachusetts. I spent four years as a state representative, ran for state senator, and eventually served as Assistant Majority Leader for the Massachusetts State Senate.

As simple and straightforward as that might sound, my journey to office was far from a straight line. After college, I went to secretarial school in order to qualify for a position I was offered by the parent of a classmate after he heard my college graduation speech. My secretarial school certificate enabled me to land a job at the Suffolk County District Attorney's office typing up criminal arraignment forms and other reports involving drug and vice cases within the city of Boston.

After a few promotions, I became a mid-level administrator, and although I had enjoyed the job, I decided to leave it in order to attend divinity school. At the same time, the First Assistant District Attorney, Newman Flanagan, recruited me to help run his campaign for district attorney. I agreed to delay my studies and run his campaign.

It was a spirited effort, with Newman and two other candidates challenging the longtime incumbent and storied national crime fighter, Garrett Byrne. Mr. Byrne was 80 years old and seeking another four-year term. This was a donnybrook campaign in Boston politics. An incumbent with three Democratic challengers meant victory for us was unlikely.

Despite the odds, we won the primary and there was no general election opponent. Newman was a first-time candidate. I was a first-time coordinator, and just 23 years old. But campaigning came natural to me. I was good at it, though I didn't know it yet.

Only days after Newman's upset victory, I was recruited to schedule the general election campaign of then-Lieutenant Governor Thomas P. O'Neill, who shared the ticket with the Democratic gubernatorial nominee Edward King. They were elected, and after serving on the transition team for Newman Flanagan, I served for the next seven years as the chief administrative officer for the Suffolk County District Attorney's office.

While working full time, I completed my studies at Harvard Divinity School and at Suffolk University Law School in the evenings, and went on to practice law. I came to view religion and law as the prototypes that organize human behavior and my study of those two subjects both complemented and integrated my understanding of self, others, and the world at large.

Despite my studies and my accomplishments, I still felt a void inside. I wanted to do something different with my training and education. I wanted to make good laws and help people. It was those desires that motivated me to run for state representative. I felt deeply that the positive change I was looking for would start with the State House.

If I could have applied for a job as a lawmaker, I would have. But I had to run for it. I viewed my campaign as one long job interview. My first campaign literature was my résumé, because early on I hadn't raised enough money to produce formal literature. Nobody knew who I was. I started knocking on doors in the snow in February. By the time the September primary rolled around, people knew me very well.

Your story will be different from mine. But, you might also find similarities. Perhaps you, too, yearn to make changes, to help people, to make a difference. You have strength at your core that is tested by the challenges everyday life brings to your doorstep, but you might not recognize yourself as strong. I wrote this book to inspire you, but also to equip you with encouragement and the right information in the hope that you can discover what comes naturally to you. You can run for public office, and you can win.

Running for office is your chance to partake in a great energy that underlies our country. When you tap into that promise, you get progress. You get dignity. You get hope and love. You drill down into the very principles America was founded on and continues to channel, and you get to enjoy the full extent of our citizenship. You also gain the privilege of representing, speaking out about, and empowering change on the issues that matter to you and to your fellow citizens.

Most candidates today differ greatly from the population as a whole. They often have little in common with the people they are charged with representing if they get elected. In the May/June 2011 issue of *Boston Review*, Stephen Ansolabehere cited a study from the Cooperative Congressional Election Study stating that one out of every 100 adults, or about six million people, have run for office at some point in their lives.[1] However, those six million people tend to be male, well off, and older, as these statistics show:

- Men are twice as likely as women to run for office.

- People with postgraduate educations are three times as likely to run as those who have only high school diplomas.

- Those who earn $100,000 a year are almost twice as likely to run for office as those who make $50,000 a year.

- Most people who run are in late middle age. Just two percent of 18 to 54 year olds have run for office.

That is the picture of who runs for office in America today. It leaves out a lot of people. Our cities and towns are filled with many diverse, committed leaders. If we want our government, our laws, and our policies to look different, we need a more revealing and authentic mix of people in the public square.

If you hold a mirror up to elected officials today, maybe you don't see yourself in the reflection. You might feel as if there is no place for you among the decision-makers.

But in order to meet the challenges our country now faces—creating more jobs or a wiser and more affordable energy policy, for example—we need all sorts of people to come together, join in conversation, and light the way.

The only requirements to hold most public offices in America are citizenship, age, and residency. It is not written in any document that you need an advanced degree, a fat bank account, or a certain background.

In America, every person counts the same. Everyone has dignity and deserves a voice. You don't need to wait until you have some magic combination of traits to step up and run; you already have them.

The true beauty of the Unites States does not reside in institutions; it lives in people. If there are changes you'd like made, don't wait for them to come from above. Look inside yourself.

Turn the mirror around and see yourself clearly: a sound decision maker, a hard worker, and a leader. This book will help you cultivate and share the qualities you already possess to more fully live your citizenship.

The Road to Candidacy Is Personal

The future belongs to those who believe in the beauty of their dreams.

—ELEANOR ROOSEVELT

Look around your community. What makes you feel good about living there? Maybe your kids go to top-notch public school. Perhaps there's a beautiful park nearby, bike paths on the main streets, or protected lands to hike through. The trash gets picked up once or twice a week, and all your recycling goes in one bin. There's a recreation center, senior center, or YMCA nearby that serves young and old alike. Maybe you feel grateful that you can walk around safely at any hour of the day.

Then again, maybe you feel disappointed and frustrated. There are parts of your neighborhood you'd like to see improved, and that deserve to be better.

Instead of hanging onto that frustration, turn your thoughts in a more positive direction. Remember, America is the oldest enduring democracy on the face of the planet. The individuals who founded our country and created our Constitution—Ben Franklin, Thomas Jefferson, John Adams—experienced a day in their lives when they stopped complaining about what they didn't like or didn't have, and decided instead to work toward change. It's in our DNA as a nation to make changes, not to complain.

Many things that are fair and right about where you live are there because someone like you decided to fight for them, and won. Public education, anti-discrimination laws, recycling, clean water, and a new bridge are all there because someone in office wanted them and then helped make them happen.

Start with the Issues that Matter to You

Deciding to run starts close to your heart and home. Most likely, you are an expert in one or two areas, stemming from education or life experience. You might sell real estate or insurance. You might be involved in your children's education or run a small business. Maybe you went to law school, or you work for a nonprofit agency or a utility company. You're a parent, or a firefighter, or you take care of a disabled relative or aging parent.

Think of that expertise as a seed, ready to grow into a larger body of knowledge. You don't need to have all the answers before you run for office. Instead, move forward holding these five tenets of running for office firm in your mind:

- I will learn from others.

- I will bring together different points of view.

- I will do my research and explain and inform my opinions.

- I will become a resource for resolution.

- I will work hard for positive change.

The best preparation for running for office is to ask, "What do I care about?" That will point to the issues you want to involve yourself with deeply and where you will initiate change. Harness the hunger you feel when you get close to issues that truly matter to you, the ones that affect your everyday life. Take that sense of calm urgency and use it to spark your campaign.

At the most basic level, you want to provide more access to the real promise that America offers each of us. You can bring that better world about, if you so choose and are willing to work for it.

Be Your Best Candidate: Questions to Ask

List three issues in your neighborhood, town, or city that are important to you.

_____

_____

_____

Why are you running for this office?

_____

_____

_____

_____

What do you think an average day of holding this office will involve?

_____

_____

_____

_____

What would you like to accomplish in this office?

_____

_____

_____

_____

_____

_____

How do you think that will be accomplished?

_____

_____

_____

_____

_____

_____

All Aboard the Campaign Express

I made my campaign announcement in West Roxbury, Massachusetts. I stood beneath a big banner with a picture of a train on it. It read, "All Aboard the Campaign Express." My family and friends were there. I was so nervous. I was a lawyer and had been a teacher and a senior-level administrator. Despite all that, I could not seem to get my little speech out of my mouth. Once introduced, I just stood there in absolute silence for many long seconds. Finally my voice came, and I said, "You all know me. I have a desire to serve and help the community. I want to make the laws fairer. I care about being responsive and responsible to you."

My decision to run for state representative was personal. I ran to support a particular issue that meant something to me: improving access to mental health care and treatment, and eliminating the stigma surrounding mental health services.

During one of my first debates as a candidate for state office, I was asked a question that concerned placing group homes for the developmentally disabled in my hometown of West Roxbury. Prior placements had not gone well and had become controversial.

After a pause, I took a deep breath and pretty much said, "There but for the grace of God go I." I said that I support group homes and mental health treatment in my community. The group home residents and the neighborhood deserve that it be done fairly and safely with appropriate placements and quality staffing.

You could have heard a pin drop in the debate venue. Then someone started to clap. More people joined in. People stood up, one by one.

Later in my career, I lived on a street with a group home for the developmentally disabled, and they were the best neighbors anyone could have.

Why Will You Run?

Now it's time for you to think about what matters most to you and figure out your own reasons for wanting to run. Will you run for school committee because you want your children to have better learning opportunities? Do you want to stop a huge mall or other overdevelopment from being built nearby, or fortify sorely needed veterans services? Perhaps you want to secure more public transportation, or explore alternative energy sources?

Think about the people you care about. Not just your family and friends, but also your neighbors, the people who live and work in your town or city.

You have a special awareness, born of your own experience, education, and values. Only you can bring that unique mix to bear on the concerns of your community, and on the policies and laws. If a problem needs to be scrutinized, clarified, and understood by a wider audience, it must be brought to the public square. And someone like you needs to place it there.

Taking your place at the table can help change the status quo. Basing your run for office on the issues that matter to you might feel small, but you'll have the chance to effect important change. When you bring caring and creativity to any job in politics, your passion renews our government, and that better serves all of us.

Be yourself, know what you're talking about, and know what you believe. Stick to those tenets. If you do, you'll be surprised at how easy it can be to overcome any amount of negativity, and replace it with positive, forward momentum.

Be Your Best Candidate: Questions to Ask

What do you expect campaigning to involve as far as:

Time commitment

_____

_____

_____

_____

_____

Activities

_____

_____

_____

_____

_____

Expenses

_____

_____

_____

_____

_____

2

It's Not Just a Job— It's a Job You Might Love

Nothing great was ever achieved without enthusiasm.
—RALPH WALDO EMERSON

My early campaign experiences taught me that you truly do attract what you send out. A candidate who sends out the best kind of positive energy will get lots of people on board. People vote for people, not political parties or sound bites. Campaign momentum starts out with a few voices and offers of support and encouragement. It can end up as a tidal wave.

Volunteers show up. They see you working hard. Their friends see them working hard, and they tell more friends. People know that if you work hard as a candidate, you will work hard when elected. If you keep at it, that energy starts to chip away at the status quo. It can make a pretty big dent if you stay with it.

I also learned we should not blindly rely on institutions. I started to see that government, church, corporations, schools, and medical systems were not always perfect, and that the people running them were not always acting in the interests of the people they were charged to serve.

Maybe you experienced a similar realization in your life, and you felt a bit out of sync with institutions you'd like to depend on. Consider that feeling a sign. Instead of resigning yourself to living in a rudderless community or unjust world, recognize that you have power. The simplest of actions can have repercussions that ripple outward to touch many people and effect change all the way to the top. Most change begins at the bottom. As a result, the people on top are often the last to get on board. But you have to make the decision to throw your rock in the pool and let it happen.

You've Already Done It

Running for and holding office is just a job. That's right, it's a job! It's not an exclusive club, and the people who do it are only human. Approach voting, volunteering, community involvement, or candidacy with a hunger for information. Bring your commitment, caring, and creativity, just like you do to the other areas of your life. You will succeed. You will be surprised. You may even love it.

You passed the real estate or civil service exam. You got registered as an architect, pharmacist, or general contractor. You have served in the military. You raised children, or taught the children of others. You wrote software, repaired computers, or built information systems for a corporation. You became a firefighter or a police officer. You ran a household. You were on the PTA board, or you were a Boy or Girl Scout leader. You started your own business. You took tests, learned regulations, underwent scrutiny from supervisors or regulatory agencies, and took continuing education courses.

Every one of these achievements qualifies you to be exactly the kind of leader your community needs. A public office isn't a monument to superior intellect, money, or power. It's an opportunity to be of service, and to grow personally. And it's a chance that's ripe to be seized.

A Bigger Reason to Run

Have you ever been visited by a difficult situation and had to work your way out of it? America is no different. Our country began when a group of people took an uncharted course, resulting in what is now the oldest and most enduring Constitution in human history.

The freedom and independence that inspired our nation burned first in the souls of its people. Our country has faced many challenges in the course of its young life: slavery, the Great Depression, World Wars, the Cold War, and the struggle for Civil Rights. In more recent times, we battled greed and banking scandals in government and in the private sector. We have witnessed ongoing healthcare inequality and a growing wage gap.

It was the early colonists' demands for economic dignity that led to the American Revolution. It is up to us to carry on that spirit, whether it is threatened from outside our borders or from within them. We don't need to take up arms as the early patriots did. But we are called upon to join the fight in another way. Today, many have a palpable feeling of discontent, a visceral sense of unfair treatment, and a vision that the scales are tipping away from equality and justice. By increasing our civic involvement, choosing the right kind of disruptive action, and instigating change, we can begin to bring things into balance.

The economic crises of the recent past were caused by people who made unwise and unjust financial decisions that led to great personal gains for a few, while many suffered. Ignoring problems like these won't make them disappear. We must seek ways to rebuild and renew in their aftermath.

The first steps toward that rebuilding are increased involvement and deeper engagement at all levels of American society. If you need a greater reason to seek public office, this is it. If more citizens run for office and win, the concerns of more Americans will be raised, discussed, and addressed. More candidates will infuse our institutions with energy, knowledge, and common sense.

Town of Bedford, Massachusetts, Government Chart

This is a typical organizational chart showing local government offices. It is a valuable tool for citizens, as well as a necessity for anyone running for a public office.

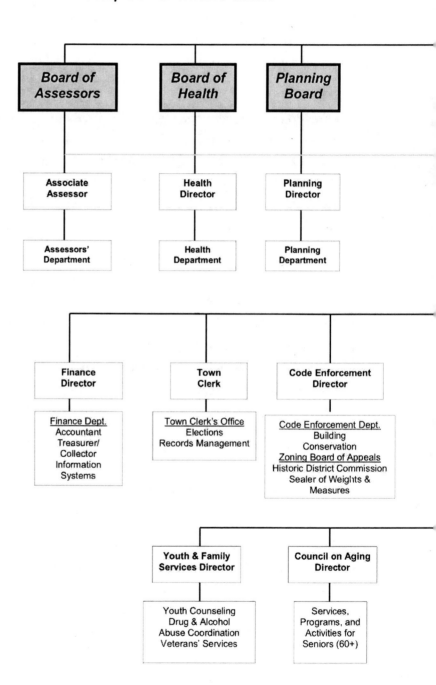

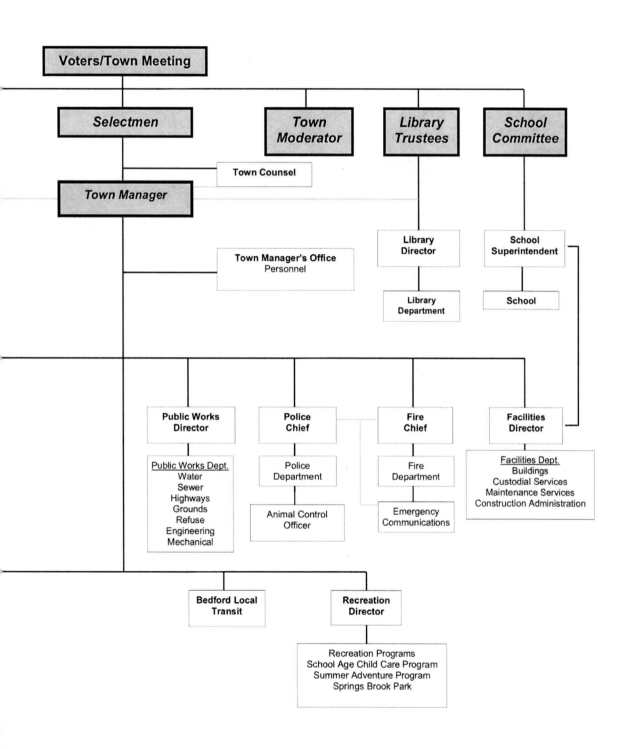

I believe that as a nation we are in the midst of a transformative life cycle, one that includes gestation and birth, growth, decline, and rebirth. Avoiding the downward slide requires more personal involvement, not less. It is productive. Try it. See what happens if 20 registered voters, ones who actually vote, call or visit an elected official with a simple request. That request will be honored. Write a letter to the editor of your local paper, or post a polite video on YouTube. Then step back and take in the positive results you ignited. Above all, register to vote, and show up at the polls at the next local or national election. Not everyone has to be more involved for great things to happen—just more of us.

Choose to run. You will bring forward a set of concerns that need attention and resolve. You might inspire others to stand beside you and lend their strength to your effort, or you could become a model for other citizens who are in doubt. Your effort will matter.

Be Your Best Candidate: Questions to Answer

What office are you running for?

_____

What skills will the office you seek require?

_____

_____

_____

_____

_____

What do you see as your strongest skills right now?

_____

_____

_____

_____

_____

_____

What skills do you need to strengthen?

_____

_____

_____

_____

_____

_____

How will you gain the skills you need and maximize the ones you already possess?

_____

_____

_____

_____

_____

_____

Preparing for Candidacy

*Never doubt that a small group of thoughtful,
committed citizens can change the world. Indeed, it is
the only thing that ever has.*

—MARGARET MEAD

Fired up yet? If all this inspirational talk has kindled a desire to serve your community in a deeper way, you're ready to run—for something. You've still got a few decisions ahead of you, and then it's on to the task of building support and momentum for your campaign. This is easy. You do it person by person, one conversation at a time. The first step is to do your research: Make sure you want to do the job you are running for. Then, determine if you can win.

What Office Should You Run For?

Explore what you care about most, then research which agency or government office has influence over the issues and policies that affect that area.

If the public pool or basketball courts in your neighborhood are in disrepair and you want them fixed, for example, you would perhaps run for a position with Parks and Recreation. If you want to see more funding for e-books or new children's books in your public library, you might run for the Library Commission. You could run for the Zoning Board, Board of Education, Board of Health, Housing Authority, Planning Board, selectman, county auditor, or state representative. Familiarize yourself with the way government and public policy works in your area, and choose the position where your skills and knowledge will be best placed.

Some elected offices are full-time, and some are part-time. Some are salaried, some have a stipend attached, and some are on a volunteer basis. Some have term limits, and some do not. You can (and should) learn about how your own town or city is organized and all the details of an office you may be interested in by going to town hall or an official municipal website.

Who Holds the Office Now?

Before you decide to run for a particular position, gather the following information:

- Is it an open seat? If not...

- When is the incumbent's term up?

- Is the incumbent popular?

- Is the incumbent performing well? Or does he or she lack engagement with the issues and constituency?

- Has the incumbent run for reelection before? Was he or she opposed?

How Do You Know if You Can Win?

First, you want to be sure that you can do that job and carry out the duties and responsibilities that go along with it. Next, take a look at the results from the last three to five elections for that office, and answer these questions:[2]

- How big was the voter turnout?

- What precincts or areas did the votes come from?

- Who voted? (What were the proportions of men, women, seniors, students, union employees, and government employees, for example?)

- How did the area, town, or precinct where you live vote?

With these answers, you will gain a sense of the possible political base for your campaign and an idea of how many votes you can hope to win.

Who Ran for this Office in the Past?

Next, analyze how prior campaigns for this office were run and how successful they were. A few questions to ask include:

- Who ran previously for this office, and how well did they do?

- What kind of campaign did they run? Was it organized, positive, and visible?

- Does the seat have a primary and/or a general election?

- Are there other big races, such as a presidential, mayoral, or congressional election, happening at the same time that might affect voter turnout? Are big ballot questions up for a vote that will draw a larger percentage of the community to the polls?

Say Hello to the Blanks!

Consider, too, the votes a candidate did not get on Election Day. "Blanks" are those instances where someone could have voted for a particular candidate, but left their ballot blank. Sometimes blanks result when people only vote for top-tier candidates and skip the lower part of the ballot. The lower a candidate is on the ballot, the more blanks he or she generally receives. Since you're likely to start off running for an office low on the ballot, there could be a sizeable number of blanks.

A voter might leave a blank when a candidate is unopposed, under the perception that their vote isn't necessary. It could be that the voter feels uninformed, or has no opinion either way about the candidate. Blanks may also show that the voter doesn't like how an incumbent is performing at the job, but wasn't impressed or knowledgeable about the opposing candidate. The understanding and interpretation of "blanks" can be unique to those candidates, that district, and that race. Generally speaking, incumbents receive about 30 percent blanks.

Take a look at how many blanks your opponent(s) received. A popular person running unopposed will get a few blanks. But a person running unopposed who gets a lot of blanks is a message you should pay attention to, because it shows there are voters out there who are dissatisfied with the status quo and might be looking for a fresh candidate to vote for.

What Is Your Online Presence?

If you have an online presence and social media engagements, these are already a part of your public profile—who you are and who you appear to be to others.

Once you decide to run for office, it is smart to conduct an exhaustive search of your name, your spouse, your children's names, your business, your business associates, and so forth to see what information may be posted about you. To be thorough, add your state and town to the search. If you come across any negative information have a plan in place to answer or explain it. Be sure to repeat some of your searches throughout your campaign.

It is usually better to conduct a search with your search terms in quotes (" ") because using quotes provides you with more accurate search results.

Social media and online presence is something to be discussed fully with your family, friends and with your campaign team as your journey progresses. If you are new to social media, their expertise could prove invaulable to your campaign.

It is also important for you to explore the online presence of other candidates. Be careful how you use any information you find; separate fact from fiction.

There are lots of people who live on social media and there are lots of people who do not. It may seem generational, with younger people more likely to have social media accounts, but the important truth is that social media has no age boundaries.

What Is the Potential Voter Universe for Your Opponent(s)?

Impartially, get a sense of your opponents' popularity and voter strength, so you know which voters are likely to support them.

I campaigned in every community and every segment of my district. I knew that certain populations—hockey parents and seniors, for example—might know and prefer one of the other candidates over me in the beginning of the campaign. I hoped that by the close of the campaign, I would earn their votes. By Election Day, they would know me. They would see that I was more qualified and committed to them and to our community. That belief underscored every interaction I had on the campaign, and informed every action I took.

Put Your Information to Work for You

Once you have secured your answers and gathered information about the opposition, calmly and quietly consider the variables. A close study of previous races for the office you plan to seek will teach you a lot about what kind of campaign you should run and your chances of winning. Also, learn about your potential opponents and examine their voter turnout strengths and weaknesses.

For example, when I ran for state representative, I saw from the voter turnout lists we had created (I will explain how to create your own in a later chapter) that one of my opponents had become un-enrolled in a political party; and had almost beat the incumbent in the last election, losing by a very narrow margin. It was not legally possible for him to enter the Democratic Party and run in the primary.

His decision to become un-enrolled in a political party had made sense at the time: He wanted to oppose the incumbent directly in the November general election, while avoiding the Democratic primary and not having to run as a Republican, which would probably not have met with success in this district. But in the interim, the landscape had changed. The incumbent did not run for his seat again. I ran, as did others, in a crowded Democratic primary field. As a result, I won the primary and the now un-enrolled candidate was facing me, rather than the entrenched longtime incumbent, as he had expected. If he had been able to enroll as a Democrat, he may have won the primary and likely would have had no opposition in the general election.

Sometimes things you cannot anticipate or control unwittingly advance your candidacy. I may not have won the primary if he had been one of my Democratic opponents. As it was, I beat him narrowly in the general election. The lesson here: Be sure to learn and follow the legal requirements associated with the office you're interested in—including those of party affiliation.

Another candidate was a high-profile city employee who worked in senior services. Her family was involved in youth hockey, she was older than me, and she had grown children. Her employment facilitated access to a large percentage of senior voters, who were important because the older electorate represented the largest voting block for the state rep's seat in my district. Plus, her family was popular and very involved in the community. So, I could see that she would potentially receive a healthy number of votes from people who knew her and her family.

Yet another opponent was a leader in the large local Catholic Church and active in the parish. That would net him a certain percentage of votes, particularly among people who attended that church.

Find out what kind of voter turnout the Secretary of State's office, media, and those who follow local politics predict, and how it will affect both you and your opposition. Remember, a large voter turnout is not necessarily friendly to incumbents, because the increased number of voters will likely include people who do not necessarily support the status quo, and who may desire change. Incumbents generally prefer low voter turnouts because they bring fewer surprises and make it more likely they will get reelected. Large turnouts, on the other hand, signify more people in the conversation, which sometimes means change is in the air. Larger than usual turnouts also usually cost more money, because more people are voting and need the candidate's attention.

It's important to be aware of what is happening in your community relative to ballot questions, override initiatives, or big political races with which you will share the ballot. These are all factors that will bring more voters to the polls and have an impact on the kind of race you must run.

What Are Your Strengths and Weaknesses?

Know yourself, too, inside and out. Honestly assess your strengths and weaknesses, advantages and disadvantages. You have a "universe," too. Understand it and it can become your greatest advantage.

- Are you well known, or is a member of your family in the public eye? Are the other candidates more or less well known than you?

- In what areas do you have influence because of your particular background, job, hobbies, or community involvement?

- Where do you and your opponent(s) differ on issues, background, and ideology? Where are you similar?

Your base starts close to home, and close to your heart. At the broad, stable bottom of your base stand the people who already know you, understand you, and like you. They can be your greatest champions, your hardest workers, and your most valued supporters. You grow outward and upward from that base. Its strength allows you to develop as a candidate and a leader. You grow from your base, and then your base grows.

When More People Run, Everyone Wins

Ask yourself: Would I vote for my opponents in this election? Would I vote for them over me, if I were impartial? Why or why not? I never viewed my campaign for office as "me" against "them." Instead, I saw other candidates as wanting the same position I wanted. I knew they had a right to run, too. This feeling of equality and friendliness fueled my thoughts and actions throughout my campaign. I told my friends, family, and supporters, when relevant, that this was my attitude.

This attitude of acceptance will carry you beyond your campaign and serve you well. Remember, all campaigns come to an end. You can win, and when you do you will be representing your opponents and their friends, not just your supporters and friends.

When I was in the company of my opponents or their supporters, I was polite and cordial. In a lively and passionate campaign, you will really get to know your opponents. You will see one another often at events. The local press will write about them and you will see their literature. Your supporters and theirs know, live, and work together, and they might trade feedback or stories. I didn't overly engage with my opponents or seek out interaction, but I didn't ignore them, either. You need to strike a balance between being either preoccupied with your opponents or denying their existence, and, thus, their dignity.

This I learned from my parents as a child: Every person is entitled to be acknowledged and respected. I urge you to live this lesson throughout your time as a candidate and office-holder. You will never find yourself dragged down into negativity when you treat others with courtesy, respect, and acceptance, whether they're opponents or supporters.

Once the campaign is done, you might be surprised how little separates you and your supporters from those who also ran. Your future support might come from corners you can't possibly foresee or expect at the outset of your campaign. Keep that in mind as you run, and build bridges rather than burn them.

Your Magic Carpet: The Belief That You Can Win

To gain the faith, trust, and votes of your constituency, you must first believe in yourself. That belief will be your magic carpet. It will lift you high as you progress along this journey through candidacy and election, and it will help you soar over problems, negativity, and doubt. If you truly believe that you have what it takes to serve, others will share the same view and walk beside you, inspired by your confidence. That magic carpet of self-belief can grow so wide and long that it can buoy up an entire community.

Each time I ran for office, I didn't know I would win. But I believed I *could* win. Deep down, I was convinced that I could triumph, if I only worked hard enough. You can, too.

The first time I ran for state rep, the seat became open because the incumbent dropped out of the race to run for another office. I ran because the incumbent had held the seat for a long time, and I honestly thought I could do a better job. I thought I had more energy and the potential to be a stronger voice for the community, which had changed greatly since the incumbent first stepped into office. I felt the people were ready for a change.

It was 1988, and I was not a well-known candidate. I lived in the smallest voting precinct in the state representative district. At the same time, the then-governor of Massachusetts from a bordering community, Michael Dukakis, was running for President of the United States as the Democratic nominee. I came from an already high-turnout, voter-rich district, but voter turnout was predicted to be even bigger due to increased awareness of the presidential campaign, and the energy surrounding political activity in my community was acute.

I had to win a primary, and then face off in a general election against a popular and qualified local attorney and military veteran who was married with children. At the time I was a single, young homeowner in the community, and also an attorney. My opponent had run for state representative before, and was defeated in the general election by a painfully close margin—fewer than 80 votes. If the same voters turned out for him in this election as did previously, I would have an even tougher race ahead of me in the general election.

When I ran for state Senate, on the other hand, I ran against an incumbent senator. He had run previously and lost only narrowly. He then ran a second time and beat the incumbent, and was completing his first term. My state representative district was only 25 percent of the state Senate district. That race was a different experience, but I ran for the same reasons.

I had to give up my state representative seat to run for state senator. I thought by serving in higher office I could accomplish more, and I did.

If you feel you'd be more effective than the person who holds the office you want to run for, if you think your voice is stronger, then do it. I did, and I won. But if you don't run, you will never win. If you don't run, you squander the chance to have a greater voice and present a more effective choice for your community.

Remember, no matter how good your competition looks, how small your base seems as you embark on your campaign, or how many naysayers tell you there's no way you'll win, there are three points you can hold up as truth throughout your campaign.

- I belong here.

- Anyone can choose to run.

- Anyone who chooses to run and wins will serve.

There's no engraved invitation on its way to your mailbox, asking you to join this conversation. The office you are running for does not belong to the incumbent, or to your opponent, or even to you when you win. It belongs to the public. That's your reason to step up, the knowledge that anyone whose true aim is to be a good leader and a dedicated public servant is the right person for the job.

Every candidate on a ballot has strengths and weaknesses, and potential waiting to be fulfilled. The ability to tap into your potential at the ballot box is the raison d'être for the campaign exercise. With it comes other positive consequences. You grow. You build community. You give your priorities and your issues a voice. You begin to personify the change you seek.

Be Your Best Candidate: Questions to Answer

An important trait for future candidates to develop is self-awareness. Start your process of self-examination early, and repeat it often. The more you understand what drives you, infuriates you, makes you happy, and puts you on the defensive, and the deeper you dig into the reasons behind your actions, positions, and feelings, the more poise and self-possession you will bring to your campaign. Here are a few questions to get you started down the road to self-discovery.

How do you respond to people who do not agree with you?

_____

_____

_____

_____

How do you respond to people who do not like you?

_____

_____

_____

_____

If someone doesn't like you, do you need to know why?
☐ Yes ☐ No

Do you view conversations as an opportunity to listen, learn, and engage?
☐ Yes ☐ No

How do you respond to people you do not like?

_____

_____

_____

_____

How do you react when someone questions your judgment or opinion?

_____

_____

_____

_____

Do you see people, issues, and points of view as "right" or "wrong?"
☐ Yes ☐ No

A Great Campaign Runs on People

We are not here to curse the darkness, but to light a candle that can guide us through that darkness to a safe and sane future. For the world is changing. The old era is ending. The old ways will not do.

—JOHN F. KENNEDY

Think back to those five crucial tenets from Chapter One. The second, "You will bring together different points of view," starts to happen the moment you decide to run and announce your candidacy.

Yes, you need to build your base. Yes, you need people to vote for you. But there's a deeper, more beautiful and worthwhile force at work here and it runs like a river beneath every successful campaign: understanding. Not agreement, not partisanship, and not coercion, but understanding. Everyone won't always agree, but you can create a culture where people are heard, respected, and understood.

As a candidate, you are given a tremendous gift—an opportunity to bring together groups of people. They may sit on opposite sides of the political fence, live in different neighborhoods, speak different languages, and come from varied cultural and religious backgrounds. It is about them getting to know you, and your getting to know them.

The issues will come and go. What matters is the respect and understanding between you and the voters, even though you may not necessarily agree on every issue. The circumstances in a person's life, in a neighborhood, and in a community may change, but the ability to contribute and lead remains constant.

When you establish this mutual respect, person by person, you build the foundation of your leadership and service. Yes, sometimes people may react emotionally to certain issues. They may wait to see where you stand. This observation might inform, energize, and refine their opinions. Then again, sometimes you won't make any headway with this voter, and you will continue to disagree. And that's okay too.

When you disagree you may think, "There goes a place to plant a house sign," or "Now they will not host the house party," or maybe "Now they will leave my campaign and go to an opponent who agrees with them." However, that never happened to me, at least that I am aware of. People appreciate your consideration and your thoughtful inquiry. They will not leave you or your campaign because you do not agree on a particular issue. As a matter of fact, every day you will meet someone with whom you do not agree. If you seek to please simply for the sake of their support, you are not being the sincere, reliable leader you want to be, or the one they want to support. Working out disagreements is part of every relationship. You can handle it in this context, too.

As you build your team and get support from your future constituents, you're going to hear many differing points of view. You will get the chance to listen to many people, to think, to come to your own conclusions, and to respond. By doing this, you will foster a greater understanding. Get a few people in a room eager to learn what you're all about, and watch it happen. You are now the voice for many, and you have an incredible journey ahead.

The Power of Coffee Hour

As far as bringing together those disparate points of view and gaining support for your campaign, a "coffee hour" or "house party" is one of your most effective tools. It happens naturally. It does not need to be, nor should it be, staged. I attended, gratefully, a few hundred coffee hours throughout my candidacies. They took place in the homes of generous people. My coffee hours happened at big split levels and small ranches in the suburbs, in urban apartments, in garages, on porches, and in living rooms, basement family rooms, and kitchens all over my district.

Every time, I kept my second tenet in mind. I was not afraid to encounter viewpoints that differed from my own. That was what my campaign was all about, hearing what people had to say, understanding what was important to them, and learning how they formed their opinions. Coffee hours were my chance to do those things.

When you're scheduling your own coffee hours for your campaign, keep these guidelines in mind to help both you and your constituents get the most out of them:

Set a plan, and follow it

Create a coffee hour protocol, and type it up for the host and the volunteers involved with the coffee hour or house party. Ask the host to invite people for 6:30 or 6:45 in the evening, for example, so they have time to arrive, settle in, and have something to eat or drink before you arrive at 7 o'clock. Make campaign materials available at the event—even if, like me, you only have a résumé or short write-up outlining your background and qualifications. Create and follow a checklist of all the duties that need to be completed to set up, run, and follow up a successful coffee hour. Take the guesswork out of the process with a system for planning and execution, and you'll be able to set one up at a moment's notice.

Take the pressure off

A coffee hour or house party offers no presumptions and absolutely no pressure. The people who show up aren't agreeing to vote for you or make a campaign contribution. There's no contract to sign, checks to write, or promises to make at one of these events. Rather, you are being given an important chance to meet and get to know voters in your district.

Let people get to know you

People who get to know you personally and experience what you are about are more likely to vote for you. That's why there are so many jokes about politicians shaking hands, kissing babies, and showing up at the local car wash or bake sale. At the base of that humor is truth: Getting yourself in front of people is absolutely key to gaining positive momentum for your campaign, and getting votes. If people like you and respect you, they will vote for you—even if they disagree with you.

Build on the connections you already have

Your coffee hours start with the people who know you best. Think of everyone you come in contact with in the course of a month. Are you in a book club? Do your children take dance lessons, play soccer, compete in the chess club, or swim at the YMCA? Are you in a garden club or cooking club? Do you have a hobby like fishing, hunting, or rebuilding engines? Are you a military veteran, do you belong to a church, or did you attend school in the area?

Every activity you enjoy is your entree into a group of potential supporters. What's more, they are guaranteed to be people who already share at least one thing in common with you, a hobby, interest, or activity. Chances are that when you dig deeper you'll find you have even more in common. People will remember those connections when they go to cast their vote.

Who is going to come to your first coffee hour? Ask one person, or more, in each of the organizations you are involved with to help you. Inquire if they'd be willing to host a coffee hour. Ask them to activate their own web of personal and professional contacts, and to introduce you to their network.

Always, always remember: If people meet you, they are more likely to vote for you.

Virtual Coffee Anyone?

You may want to consider "virtual" coffee hours, in addition to your in-person appearances. This is a tool that may be appropriate under certain circumstances, for example, a scheduled coffee hour is planned, but you had been traveling and your flight was cancelled because of a storm.

Or the host prefers a "virtual" coffee hour and it works best for her and her guests. Generally speaking, in person, live and on the ground are the most effective and enduring approaches to meet and connect with others. However, alternative platforms can be effective and welcome to the host and guests.

A Candidacy Is Based on Connection

Your coffee hour will be more effective if you can gather together as many people as possible. Remember, every person who attends possesses their own network of connections, and if they like what they hear and see and feel at a coffee hour, they are more likely to spread the word about you. Imagine if each guest tells two people, and then they each tell two people. It's powerful.

Depending on the space available, I recommend inviting as many people as the host's comfort level allows. Many people will decline because of schedule conflicts or disinterest, especially early in the campaign. However, that's likely to change. Near the end of my campaign, I had more coffee hour opportunities than could be scheduled.

Every coffee hour I attended was unique. Attendance ranged from 12 to 50 people. Sometimes, it was in the living room with sweets and coffee. At other times, it was a barbecue or a pool party—whatever worked for the host worked for me.

While a general rule for coffee hours is, the more people the better, smaller parties matter, too. In fact, you sometimes have deeper and wider conversations and gain bigger commitments to your campaign when there are fewer people at the event.

Ask someone other than the host to be your helper at the event. Your helper, usually a campaign volunteer, arrives early to help set up. He or she can also arrange for guests to sign in to the event with names, e-mail addresses, home addresses, and phone numbers. You want to be free to engage personally with the guests at a coffee hour, but it's also important that you collect this information, so ask for help with the logistics.

Think about what you want to say at a coffee hour, but avoid writing a scripted speech. Your main objective is to have the event be natural and comfortable. People will know immediately if you are reticent or if it's too orchestrated, and it will put you and them off. Be yourself; carry your leadership role models in your heart and your mind's eye. Your main purpose here is to connect personally with people.

Those personal connections can come from surprising and unlikely places. You talk with someone and find out you both use the same plumber or local tree service. You both love bluegrass music, or documentaries, or trail running. Your kids go to the same school, play in the same sports league, or were both on the debate team. You got married in the same church.

Don't forget: You've done this before. You've entered a social event and talked to people you didn't yet know, and you came to understand, respect, and like them, and they you. You made friends, business contacts, and social connections. Coffee hours can be very similar to these kinds of scenarios, except you are approaching them as a candidate.

Learn from Your Future Constituents

Now, it's around 7:30 p.m. It is time for you to stand up and speak to your coffee hour guests. Explain how happy you are to be there, how grateful you are to the host(s) for offering their home and time and good effort. Your hosts are putting their reputation on the line for you in a way by agreeing to do this, so acknowledge it as the big deal that it is.

I usually spoke for about 20 minutes at a coffee hour. I always said, "I'm here to meet you, get to know you; I hope that you get to know me."

I would tell them my story. I told them where I grew up, a little about my parents and their roots, about my education and professional experience and accomplishments. I was conversational and tailored my comments for the specific group. However, I tried to connect with people and explained that I wanted to help make good laws, safer neighborhoods, and better schools. I saw those talks as a way to forge connections with the people who shared my neighborhood, to help them see that their hopes, concerns, and fears were the same as mine. I wasn't asking for their vote, or their money. I was letting them know who I was and leaving the decision up to them.

I only asked two things of the guests: that they vote in the upcoming election and that they give me their consideration.

At the close of my remarks, I would invite questions, and respond as best I could. The host would bring the coffee hour to a close and have me wrap up, and then I would thank everyone and leave. Usually, I had another event to attend, people to telephone, or a letter to write or sign. My helper would remain and gather the materials. Often a guest would offer to host another coffee hour, and that would be gratefully arranged and scheduled.

Most people who come to your coffee hour will simply be curious. They'll be happy to find out how much they have in common with you.

That's what comes out of a coffee hour: connection. You're not there to convince people you are right, or that you know more or have the answer to everything.

You're just there to meet them. Your goal is to build upon the community you already share.

Coffee hours and other community events are also a wonderful chance to meet and recruit potential campaign volunteers. As you are introduced to a widening group at coffee hours and other events, don't be surprised if some guests step forward to help. This kind of momentum is extremely welcome—it's the way you will grow your campaign and build your organization.

Questions Are Questions

From time to time someone will ask you a tough question or invite some controversy at a coffee hour or other event. Questions are questions, not threats, even if they are presented in a tone that's less than nice. Don't let questions get you rattled, even if you don't know the answer.

When someone asked me an unexpected and difficult question at a coffee hour, I would sometimes inquire, "That is interesting. Are you comfortable sharing why that's important to you?" Then, I would simply listen.

Inviting questioners to express why something matters to them helps you understand their interest to orient your thinking. It gives you some breathing room. It diffuses any tension behind the question. Most importantly, it takes the pressure off and turns a potential disagreement into a learning opportunity for you. Most of the time, people are pleased that you want to hear what they think. If they were feeling a little upset, explaining their concerns diffuses that emotion. It also takes pressure off your host, who might feel uncomfortable or embarrassed if guests are hostile or difficult. You want everyone to know all is well.

Your job in these instances is often simply to listen. Then, know what you are talking about before you respond. You can't read people's minds, and people don't expect you to be a psychic. It's always fine to acknowledge that you do not know enough about a certain subject. Ask the person to explain it to you, and promise you'll get more information to inform your own thoughts and actions, and that you'll get back to them with an answer if necessary.

I used to debate myself, so I could poke holes in my own arguments and know what to do when people challenged my position on an issue. Practice your position statements so you know what to say when someone asks you a tough question or brings up a difficult issue, so you can stay calm and stick to the facts. Also, realize that sometimes people are just going to disagree with you, and they might be upset that you don't think the same way they do. I used to say: "I know that you are disappointed that we are not in agreement. I value your opinion, and I want to understand your perspective and help you understand mine."

The coffee hour and other events are your campaign and time in office in microcosm. Some people in the room are your friends and agree with you completely. Some aren't, and never will. Many people have strong opinions. Dealing with situations where people disagree with and even dislike you is part of being in public service. It will continue to happen when you win. Nothing happens at coffee hour or on the campaign trail that won't happen while you're holding office. Running is like one enormous job interview, and the best training session you could ask for as you prepare to serve.

Be Present

At every coffee hour and campaign event, whoever is there, be there in that moment with that person, 100 percent. Campaigns are crazy, and that chaos will become your new normal. It is up to you to be the eye of the storm, and foster positive connections with others no matter how hectic things get.

While on the campaign trail you might face distractions. You might find yourself navigating a difficult press story about you. A good friend of yours could be campaigning for your opponent because they are doing a business deal together. Your mother may have been diagnosed with breast cancer, or your teenage child could be having trouble in school. In the meantime, you must keep attending coffee hours, marching in parades, showing up to community events, explaining yourself, listening—and smiling.

Life happens, and it doesn't stop while you run for office. And guess what? Life marches on for your volunteers, the voters, and the other candidates running this race alongside you. You are all in the same boat.

The solution? Recognize every person you meet as someone who matters. Not just the people whom you already love, know, and respect, but everyone—the cashier who rings up your groceries, the cab driver who got you to your event on time, the wait staff at the restaurant where you and your volunteers held your last meeting. They all matter the same. Be present and open to the opportunity interacting with them presents. Candidates, office holders, and voters alike—we are all part of humanity. Accept it, acknowledge it, and embrace it. You may find that the difficulties suddenly seem less significant. In any case, they will pass. They always do.

During my campaigns, as during every candidacy, there were births, deaths, illnesses, unemployment, hard times and good times. Keep your balance, and remember that everything that you experience enriches your leadership skills, ferments your character, and strengthens your ability to lead and serve.

Listen to your inner voice. Take each step happily, even if sometimes it is scary.

After a while, one step at a time, you progress, and things start to take shape, and it feels normal. You develop a new normal, just as you have with other positive changes in your life. It does get easier and even more comfortable. Remember, the new normal.

There Is No "Land of Dropped Balls"

Yesterday is gone. Tomorrow has not yet come. We have only today. Let us begin.

—MOTHER TERESA

I used to say the phrase "there is no Land of Dropped Balls" all the time on the campaign trail, and my supporters knew I meant it. Coffee hours and other campaign events only work if you do the follow-up. People need to know that you are aware of their interest and support, and that you are grateful.

People will do more if they connect to your campaign on a personal level and feel respected. When people want to help, don't leave them hanging. Follow-up must be completed within 24 hours after a person expresses any sort of interest in assisting you. Supporters have many other things to do with their time. Prove you value their time and commitment and show you appreciate their support as a true and heartfelt gift.

Assembling the Team

Every campaign is different and unique, just like a romance. In my instance, my closest relatives and dearest friends thought that I could do it, but hoped I would resist. Other candidates, perhaps you, are encouraged to run by your closest circle, or you may even be recruited. The bottom line is that you must really want to serve, to learn how to run, and to be the best candidate possible. I did.

You can't do it alone. People close to me saw my commitment, and they began to help in practical ways. They, like me, cared deeply about our community, state, and country.

My older cousin through marriage, Tommy Cloherty, loved politics and was very close to my parents. He lived in Roslindale, in Sacred Heart Parish where I was born and where I had attended some elementary school. Tommy was a "hail fellow well met" person, and he wanted to run my campaign. He believed in me and thought that we were a good combination, him with his "street smarts" and he used to say about me "I would work them to death," meaning my opponents.

Tommy was a natural, a magnet. He had a flexible work schedule, and he loved people. We agreed early on that I would make the big decisions and that I would have veto power on campaign matters. I was "the boss." There was no power struggle. It also was important to me to create a campaign texture and culture that welcomed everyone. There would be no cliques. Tommy brought in his close friend, Ed Roth, and their personal circle, and they worked hard and always saw the big picture while paying attention to details.

Tommy and I spoke daily and had breakfast together many times a week early in the morning. We met one another's friends and neighbors. Out of that group, the campaign team started to emerge.

Our mutual family and friends staffed the headquarters and prepared and kept the office schedule. They brought in borrowed furniture, appliances, homey touches, and smiles. Friends and relatives brought in their friends and relatives in turn. They would express specific volunteer interests and availability, and would fill out our homemade volunteer cards. From this initial group, we found:

- Drivers for events and campaign stops who would pick me up and bring me home. (We felt it best that when campaigning, I should not drive myself, so that I could listen to updates, read material, and not be worried about where to park the car.) They would also sometimes make important deliveries to other people in the campaign, etc.

- Head of volunteers. Initially, this was my sister, Madeleine. We lived together at the time. She was spontaneous and hit the ground running, just by being her natural creative leader. She built a team of volunteers with leaders for most campaign projects. People loved her.

- Head of literature drops. This was my close friend and neighbor, Paul McLaughlin. Paul and the Head of Volunteers organized all of our drops, usually three or four for each campaign. "Literature drops" are when volunteers deliver campaign literature to the homes of voters. They save you money on postage, help you build your campaign organization, and teach you about each neighborhood in the community you hope to serve.

- Head of phone banks. This was Vin Buchanan, who was active in the community and a good friend of Tommy Cloherty. Vin and my friend Beth Mullaney did all of the phone bank leadership at night and on weekends because they had full-time jobs.

- Sign building and installment teams. We had wonderful sign builders and installers, with Frank Gallagher, Jack Tobin, Michael Kilgannon, Joe Abber, Ed Hardy, and many others who were friends and neighbors. It was a great help that they had tools for building and trucks for transport. The sign building, erecting and maintaining, and then taking down and storing operation was ongoing

- Door-knocking support. Early on, my close friend and a young senior, Margaret Gallagher, would pack a cooler with lunch, water, tea, and fruit. Our door-knocking team grew quickly, with Vin Buchanan, Mike Leonard, Jimmy Sutton, and retired Judge George Sullivan as the MVPs.

- Other volunteers. People signed up for regular duty to man the headquarters and attend mailings, especially my "cousins" Maureen Hegarty and Patsy Fagan, my Aunt Christina Carty, and my friend Dottie Traverse. Supporters loaned us gas grills and other supplies, and started to make and bring food to headquarters to feed the volunteers. Others, like Olie Melvin, submitted sincere and well-written letters to the local paper supporting my candidacy or refuting a criticism. As more and more people came on board, their names and information went into the computer database.

The Sunday Morning Meeting

I depended on the volunteers in charge of follow-up to ensure that my campaign would never live in "The Land of Dropped Balls." In the beginning, the head of volunteers came to a meeting at my house most Sunday mornings, as did every key member of my campaign team.

In order to run an effective campaign, all the different parts must be integrated with the whole. You, as the candidate, must be aware of what's happening (and not happening) in all quarters generally. It is your reputation and your brand that is either enhanced or undermined by even the smallest actions taken by others.

At my dining-room table most Sunday mornings sat the heads of volunteers, mailings, literature drops, visibilities, phone banks, and campaign headquarters. At our first Sunday meeting we started with primary day and worked backward to make a schedule for each week leading up to the election. At subsequent Sunday meetings we hammered out the details then and there. *What standouts do we have coming up this week? How many people do we need there?* We'd draw a map of the area and assign people to invite the volunteers.

We would take inventory. We'd go over how many new volunteers had signed up with the campaign. I'd find out how many coffee hours we had scheduled, and in which precincts. I knew which precincts had the most volunteers, and which had the least. I knew where we had people scheduled to help out on primary day, and where we needed more help. My campaign had constant accountability and transparency about where we stood, from top to bottom. We were mindful of how many weeks remained. This broke things down to small manageable pieces, and greatly eliminated our finding ourselves in the dreaded Land of Dropped Balls.

You will make your own decisions about what positions and people are key to your individual campaign, and about who needs to be at your weekly meetings, and whom you need to meet with more frequently to stay updated and avoid "dropped balls." You might decide to create a dedicated campaign position for an information technology/social media/computer expert who can help manage your social media presence and ensure databases, Websites, and other technological aspects of your campaign are in order, for example. Think about the positions you need to fill and the help you require to run a successful campaign, and be clear about those needs. The right people will come.

Don't Let That Ink Dry

As you hold coffee hours, fundraisers, and other events, you will meet the volunteers who will grow your campaign. Use whatever system works for you, paper or electronic, to sign up people who are interested in volunteering. My campaign used volunteer cards.

At coffee hours and other events early in my campaign, I asked everyone who attended to write his or her name, address, and telephone number(s) on an index card. (In later races I asked for their email addresses too.) I asked them to write down ways they could potentially volunteer for our campaign. I also asked them to type up a list of anyone that they knew who might want to be involved with the campaign, and with their permission, I would telephone their list of people. I let them know that effort would be a huge gift.

These cards and lists helped me meet an important goal: to sign on three or four new volunteers per day. The "volunteer cards" were index card size, so they could be tucked in a pocket or purse. At first they were just blank cards I'd bought at an office supply store. But later on I had cards printed with a place for the person's contact information and checkboxes that indicated what they might like to volunteer for.

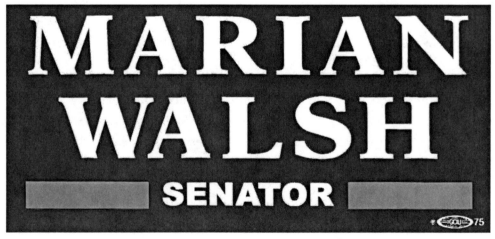

Volunteer card and bumper sticker[3]

A volunteer could offer to put one of your signs on his lawn or a bumper sticker on her car. Volunteers can make telephone calls, clean and staff campaign headquarters, bake cookies, host coffee hours, and work at the polls. There's no shortage of volunteer duties, and you'll need as many volunteers as possible. There is always more work to do, and having many people working as a team makes a campaign more fun.

Sometimes people wrote notes, volunteering for a category not on the card. For example, some people wrote that they spoke Greek or Spanish and would translate for possible radio ads or letters to voters in these communities. I took them up on these offers, and found they were very effective ways to reach these voters and build the campaign in these communities. Other people wrote they would be interested in bringing food to the headquarters for the volunteers. I took them up on these offers as well, saving money and also helping to build a sense of family among the volunteers.

Make sure you have plenty of volunteer cards available for people to fill out at your coffee hours, and everywhere else, too. People will like you and be impressed by what you say, and in that moment of trust and acceptance they will want to fill out one of those cards.

You may choose to make your own volunteer cards with your computer and printer or get them printed professionally. If the latter, choose a union print shop if having the union bug on your campaign materials is important in the areas where you are campaigning. You might want to print them on recycled paper. The choices you make in producing and printing your volunteer cards and other materials depend on you, your district, and your candidacy. At different times, I did all of the above.

Early in my first campaign all I had was my résumé, blank index cards and blank thank you notes. Later I had professionally printed materials, including campaign literature and bumper stickers. I also had a professional photograph taken that I used in campaign literature and for the media.

MARIAN
WALSH
SENATOR

Leading the Way.
Vote on Nov. 7

www.marianwalsh.com

Marian Walsh is leading the way for us.

Leading the way for accountability
- Marian spearheaded the effort for an independent review board to investigate practices and responsibilities in constructing Boston's Big Dig.
- She sponsored the bill requiring all public charities to disclose their financial statements, including religious nonprofits.

Leading the way in healthcare
- Marian pressed for landmark legislation that guarantees health insurance to most Massachusetts residents, and championed an increase in funding for substance abuse treatment programs.

Leading the way on wages
- Marian worked to raise the minimum wage in Massachusetts from $6.75 an hour to $8 by 2008 for almost 150,000 full-time workers.
- She voted against a retroactive capital gains tax unfair to middle-class property owners, which was subsequently repealed.

Leading the way in education
- Marian worked to increase education funding across the state by $210 million.
- She supported a $1 million funding increase to the Head Start program, and helped increase special education funding by $6.6 million.

Leading the way for veterans
- Marian strongly supported legislation for property tax relief for spouses of those who died in combat.
- She helped pass a law to increase annuity benefits for disabled combat veterans.

The daughter of a retired public school teacher and a medical doctor, Democrat Marian Walsh has served as state senator since 1993, and was state representative from 1989 to 1992. She is a graduate of Ursuline Academy, Newton College of the Sacred Heart, Harvard Divinity School, and Suffolk University Law School. Marian and her husband Paul live in West Roxbury.

MARIAN WALSH

Senator for Suffolk and Norfolk District

 Paid for by The Walsh Committee

Campaign literature for campaigning while serving

Take a Good Shot

A good campaign photograph is very important, both in color and black and white. It becomes your face and your image throughout the campaign and beyond. And with social media the opportunity to optimize positive campaign images is unlimited, affordable and time effective.

This can be expensive, but it's a cost you are likely able to avoid. I was fortunate to have a close friend and campaign volunteer as my campaign photographer: Frank Carpenito. He was also a Boston police detective, and the Boston Homicide Unit photographer. Frank would always tell me how happy he was to be taking the photograph of a live subject!

Campaign photo

Early on when possible he would trail me, and discreetly and gently snap photo after photo of me and other people on the campaign trail. These we placed in the headquarters window, and people would stop and enjoy all day long. Sometimes people would look for themselves and loved ones. I would provide them as gifts of gratitude with thank you notes, and they were really appreciated, and generated positive energy while building community within our campaign. Another campaign volunteer, Mark Kenny, created a campaign video from the images and we all enjoyed it at a victorious election night.

Frank was a consummate professional, and he made me relax and feel no pressure while he took the images, and his photographs were always flattering because I was comfortable with his manner, skill, and judgment.

The Magic Elastic

But receiving a filled-out volunteer card is far from the end of the interaction. Put someone in charge of following up with every person who filled out a volunteer card, and make sure they do so within 24 hours. My head of volunteers or a member of the volunteer committee would call each and every person who had filled out one of those cards to let them know how thrilled I was about their support.

These follow-up calls are also the time to learn about the potential volunteer's preferred activities and level of involvement For example, someone who is retired most likely has more time on his or her hands than a working mother who has small children. People might check off "bumper sticker" or "yard sign" because they are busy or have extenuating circumstances keeping them from doing more. A short conversation with a real, caring person from your campaign can make all the difference.

What will you learn from these follow-ups? A stay-at-home mom would love to help at campaign headquarters or host a coffee hour, if only you could find another volunteer to babysit her children. Another volunteer really wants to help and has free time, but doesn't drive. Someone else wants to host a coffee hour, but works two jobs and doesn't have time to do the work to set one up. Offer a ride or some help, and you've got yourself a committed volunteer. The volunteer in charge of follow-up should also enlist and monitor the aid of other volunteers to enter new volunteer information and details into the campaign computer database.

Your goal with coffee hour follow-up calls is to thank people and support the volunteer sign-up process. Find out what people need, assess their comfort level, and meet them where they're at. Person by person, your volunteer network grows and you soon have a committed group of people connected to your campaign. My list of campaign volunteers swelled to more than 2,500 because we were grateful and happy for the support. It becomes your magic elastic, getting bigger and wider and stronger.

Just Like Mom Said: Write Your Thank-You Notes

Once the follow-up calls were completed for the day, I would spend time writing thank-you notes. I would write a personal thank-you note to the coffee hour host, and also sign a letter for each person who attended, thanking them for coming and for their consideration. (I continued to review and personally sign each letter sent under my signature my entire time in public office.) Also, a volunteer card was enclosed for them to offer to a friend or neighbor if they were already on board. These volunteer cards had my home address on the blank side, so people could simply drop them in the mail after filling them out and so they would know they came straight to me.

Although email thank-you notes are more cost effective and more speedy than a traditional thank-you note, I urge you to resist, if possible, in your candidacy. A thank-you note, to me is almost sacred, and whatever more time and cost is involved in a non electronic format was worth it to me. This is your decision, like so many others. Just be thoughtful and think this through, so it is in fact a decision about you and your candidacy, and not only a convenience or something else. It is always about the voter, about the volunteer and the appreciation you express to them for their support of you.

If a guest had already indicated they would support me, I wrote a different message, thanking them for their commitment. This was a simple process, and it was ongoing. I did it every morning and every night. Remember the manners your parents probably taught you about sending thank-you notes. They were on to something! People will feel honest pride when they get a personal note from you, and they will remember it.

Perhaps a New Great Equalizer: Social Media

People vote for people they trust, but they also vote based on the opinions of others whom they trust. It is important for you not to discount the ability of social media to help you campaign. When you, the candidate, and those who support you, develop a strong social media presence with an engaged tribe, you can bolster your candidacy by sharing and voicing their support. The creative and smart use of technology in your campaign can help you save money and make the resources you have more impactful. The ability to get your message out and raise your visibility via social media sites, post a message on a video sharing site, ask for donations via the Web, and send a text, tweet, or an email to groups enables you to reach more people more quickly than ever before in campaigning.

A strong, positive social media and Web presence can help you communicate, grow your organization, recruit volunteers, bring in donations, and spread your message to a wide audience without spending a lot of money. You can use technology to make your own professional-looking literature and yard signs, collect and maintain voter registration and donation data, create posters and invitations to events, and record audio and video messages that can then be disseminated via the Internet. The value of this kind of technology, particularly to a small, local campaign, cannot be overstated, and can narrow the wealth gap that can exist between candidates.

The key is to use technological resources well and wisely. Keep in mind that images and words spread widely via the Internet at lightning speed, and can be misconstrued if you are not careful. Use the same care and common sense in creating and maintaining your online presence as you do when you appear in-person in public. If this is not your strong suit, and even if it is, seek out people who have technology expertise and experience, and make them part of your team so they can support your campaign in this important area.

The Right People Show Up

When you first start out, you might only have one or two people on your management team. But you still need to meet regularly in person to communicate, plan, and update. As the team grows, and it will, choose your closest collaborators carefully. Don't force a match between campaign needs and people. That approach will backfire, and you will risk hurting both your relationships and the campaign.

Instead, have faith that the right people will show up to fill in where you need them. Your skills and strengths emerge as you grow confident in your candidacy. Your supporters will grow and develop in their own right. Through that growth, they will learn where their best place is on your team. People will double and triple up on projects until the right fit develops, and the right people will fill in the right jobs. Keep your mind open and be alert for the right people. They come, sometimes from the most unexpected places. That is one of the most rewarding aspects of being a candidate, the exchange of energy that happens between you, your committed supporters, and the voters.

A Family Grows: Precious Volunteers

I was so fortunate to be bolstered by hundreds of committed volunteers and supporters during my campaigns and my time in office. I could have accomplished nothing without the friends and neighbors who became my biggest campaign supporters and most committed volunteers.

Perhaps like you, I was not political prior to my candidacy. The people who helped me were not political, either. As a matter of fact, the established political activists were behind other candidates and other campaigns, and they did not give my candidacy much consideration.

Instead, my support grew day by day from the neighborhoods where my supporters lived, worked, and voted. Around kitchen tables, at counters in coffee shops, over backyard fences, my support grew person by person. We were seamlessly connected by our romance with America, and our belief in her promise and blessings sustained us. We are grateful Americans, and that gratitude created a desire in us to fully participate in the fabric of our community and government. We achieved that aim through and with one another.

In time, the ranks of volunteers on my campaigns grew to more than 2,500. Election night was just the beginning, not the end, of our journey. Through my entire time in office, our political family continued to grow, mature, and adapt. It was a fluid network of people fueled by ideas and commitment.

While I held office, my accomplishments were possible only because those volunteers were watching my back, cheering me on, paying attention to my activities, and informing my positions. Sometimes we did not agree. I explained myself, and I listened. We learned from one another. We were a team.

Your Team Will Grow

Your team will develop and grow, too. That is the only possible outcome when you are an authentic, grass-roots candidate who truly wants to serve your community. As you travel the campaign trail, remember to keep an open mind about people who might clear the road for you. Right now, you might wonder where your great campaign staff, or professional staff when you are in office, will come from. I am a witness to the fact that the right people will appear.

Also keep in mind that you are often the only one who can head off certain problems before they start. Regular meetings, whether two people or a dozen sitting around the table, infuse those who help you with the energy and good feelings you bring to the campaign, and to receive theirs. This is your chance to make expectations clear, set the tone, and start bringing together those sometimes different viewpoints that strengthen and energize your campaign. Constantly take the vital signs of your campaign and gauge the energy level. A campaign that is moving forward and energized is a winning one.

When I won my first election for state representative, there were more than 17,600 votes cast. I won by just 1,166.[4] Remember, you won't win every vote. You just need *enough* votes. Stellar follow-up with every good voter that you or your campaign comes in contact with can help you earn those votes, person by person.

All of these steps may seem simple. They're certainly not the kind of information that makes it into most media accounts of politics. But they are the nuts and bolts of running for office. This is how I got started, by simply connecting with one person at a time. If you think of it that way, "person by person," the idea of building campaign support and garnering votes isn't so intimidating. And it works.

Campaigning in the Community

I suppose leadership at one time meant muscles, but
today it means getting along with people.
—MAHATMA GANDHI

To ready yourself for campaigning in the community at large, you must get your hands on good voting lists. Good, reliable, up-to-date voting lists are essential to your campaign. A "good" list is one that includes registered voters who consistently vote in the election for the office that you are running. Election results are maintained and certified by the office of the Secretary of State in each state. In addition, municipal and local offices also maintain election records. They are public record, and you should be able to access them.

Be sure to secure all the information you can about the people on the list, including telephone numbers and email addresses. This contact information is key because it will become the basis for your direct mailings, emailing, texting, telephone calls, polling, literature drops, and door-knocking. It will keep you from wasting people's donation dollars or your time by focusing campaign efforts on people who won't vote or who won't vote for you.

Creating a Good Voter List

There's an art to creating your "good voter list." Every community has resident lists, sometimes called voter lists. You have the right to see them and even keep a copy for yourself, but in most cases you have to pay for them. However, this list won't tell you which residents voted previously in the election in which you are running.

Local municipal offices maintain lists of "good voters," rather than just residents or voters. They are a public record as well. However, the offices are not required to give the public a list of residents who vote, or who vote in certain elections for certain races. While they are obligated under the law to collect and store this information, and the public has a right to view it, you can't save it electronically to your laptop and take it home. In many cases, you can't photocopy it either.

We created our good list manually, person by person, by visiting the town halls in our district. In each municipality, we asked to see the lists for a particular precinct and ward.

Voter Lists for Purchase

There are bipartisan and partisan groups and political parties that sell voting lists, and there are political list brokers. You can also purchase voting lists online. One such Internet site is http://www.campaignsandelections.com/resources/political-pages

Making Friends at Town Hall

In every town hall across the district, we encountered a different culture. Some supported Democratic candidates, while others leaned more Republican. Town halls in the suburbs might have been wary of me, as a candidate from the city of Boston. I found that communities usually favor the hometown candidate, and that often there was an urban-suburban tension. I wanted to ease that, both as a candidate and once elected. I was mindful that many suburban voters had city roots but did not necessarily favor a city candidate. It was very important for the voters to know that I would be available to all the voters of my district, not just the voters in the city where I lived. No doubt you want the voters to feel the same way.

I didn't want to make any waves. I went in with gratitude for their accommodation, rather than the attitude that I could ask for whatever I wanted. This isn't just a chance to get information and build good lists. It's a time to start building mutual, trusting relationships with the communities that will someday be in your constituency as an office holder. Always be concerned about how they feel and where they are coming from, rather than focusing on how much work you have to do.

At Boston City Hall, officials provided us with a table and two chairs. A rotation of volunteers sat at that table in Boston City Hall for many weeks, one quietly reading voter names off the list the officials gave us, the other checking off the name on the residents' lists that I had purchased. By hand, with a ruler, line-by-line, we created our own good voter lists for 20 city precincts.

You may not need to go through such a rigorous process, but you do need to find a way to create a good list that contains the information you need. Once you create it, keep updating it constantly. Every election, volunteers were assigned to be poll checkers. The municipality is required to allow citizens to be present and record who votes, as long as one does not disrupt the voting-day proceedings. Your poll checkers are at the voting place to update your voting list. It is a living document, and it will direct the bulk of your campaign efforts. That list ensures you are putting your energy in the areas where you are likely to earn the most votes.

Once you've got your list, place it under lock and key—it's pure gold. Among many other things, your list will keep you from wasting your time when you go door-knocking, direct mailing, and phone calling because you will only reach out to people who are likely to vote. You need to get to the folks who voted for the office that you are running for in a few prior elections. Go to the voters who vote.

People Vote

These voter lists will drive your campaign efforts in the community. Remember, it is also never too early to start considering voter registration. When you have a helper follow up with coffee-hour guests who offered to host an event or volunteer in another capacity, it's vital to confirm their name on those voter registration lists. Are they registered to vote? If they are, are they an active voter who participates in the kind of election in which you are running?

Learn the voter registration procedures and protocols in your community. Voter registration procedures dictate how early people can vote before primary or election day, when they can register, and how they are allowed to vote (online, by mail). These regulations vary widely from place to place. Specific voting rules apply to absentee voters, military personnel, the disabled, the elderly in assisted-living facilities, and other populations. Familiarize yourself with the rules and laws, so that you can assist your future constituents in the registration and voting process. I kept a copy of the voting laws in my purse and posted it on the wall at campaign headquarters. You may want to place them on your website, and find your own ways to make it as easy as possible for people to learn about registration and voting.

Let people know that the most important way they can help you is to register to vote and encourage everyone they come in contact with to do the same. If your supporters are not registered voters, the linchpin of their support is missing.

Assisting people with voter registration and absentee ballots can gain you valuable votes you might otherwise lose. In fact, I believe that I won my first race because I received the lion's share of the absentee ballot votes, which came from my many visits to area nursing homes. They made all the difference for me.

On the Trail

Once you have your lists in order and your voter registration efforts begin to mobilize, it's time to head out to campaign. Meeting people often means going to their homes. Get out your comfortable shoes and your sun hat, and pack provisions and a package of dog biscuits to pacify nervous canines. It's time for door-knocking!

I started door-knocking in the February snow for a September primary. I only knocked on the doors of people who had voted in a state primary. I knew who they were because of those useful voter lists. I knocked also during one of the hottest summers on record in Massachusetts, and it made a difference. I was out, meeting voters where they live, in unforgiving heat and stopping to change into a fresh blouse in the back of my car. Most of my opponents did much less door-knocking than I, or none at all, because of the heat. So when I door-knocked, it made more of an impact.

When door-knocking (and in my other campaign efforts), I asked people for their "consideration," not their vote. Voting is very personal, and for many people a profoundly private matter. The voters control when and if they will share who they will vote for, or who they voted for in the past. They may not feel comfortable sharing their voting choices with even their closest friends and family members, much less a stranger at the door. Sometimes people would say outright "I will vote for you," but I didn't confront or push for that answer. However, if things went well at the door and I sensed a level of support and comfort, I'd ask if the voter felt comfortable putting up a house sign or putting a bumper sticker on their vehicle.

"When You're Smiling, the Whole World Smiles with You"

If you forget everything else I say in this section about campaigning in the community, remember the one thing that's more important than anything else: smile. Smile all the time. Turning up the corners of your mouth can boost everyone's spirits, and even improve your own attitude on a tough day of door-knocking. Plus, a friendly smile puts people at ease the moment they open their door to you. After a while, that smile becomes your constant companion. It boosts your energy level, and the energy of others will rise up to meet it.

Door-knocking can be grueling—you are subject to the weather, fatigue, and, sometimes, unfriendly people. But, with the right preparation and mindset, you can do it well. On a full day of door-knocking, I would visit about 70 to 80 houses.

Anybody Home?

Know your constituency and be sensitive to their needs. For example, if I was knocking on doors during dinnertime, I was aware of it and apologized. In most cases, people did not mind. If they did, it seemed that they did not answer the door. In that case, I would write "NH" for "not home" beside the voter name on my list. That indicated I was at their home and they did not answer. I kept daily track of how many "not homes" I encountered.

When there was no answer at the door I would leave behind a personal note on my literature. I would write:

> Hello, I came by to see you today. I am running for state representative, and I would be grateful for your consideration. Thank you very much.
>
> Very truly,
>
> Marian

I quickly learned it took too much time to write these notes while standing on people's doorsteps, and that it was too messy. My sister Madeleine and I started writing out these notes at night at home, folding them neatly in thirds. Eventually, campaign volunteers wrote them in my campaign headquarters, and I would pick them up each day.

Be Your Best Candidate: Checklist ☑

When you get ready to door-knock the first few times, use this checklist to help you prepare.

Before you head out

☐ Plan where you will visit based on your voter lists.

☐ Know your route and know who lives where (students, seniors, supporters of your opponents, young families).

☐ Prepare what you want to say once the door is opened; I would smile, and offer a good morning or good afternoon. "I am Marian Walsh and I am running for state rep., I came by to say hello and ask you to consider me." Usually, the voter would open the door, see my button and realize why I was there before I said a word. They would lead the banter and I would respond accordingly. I felt comfortable and grateful to meet them. Sometimes we would discuss people we had in common and let things just develop in a natural way as one person talking to another. I passed my campaign materials to them, and after the door closed, I would record on the voter list my assessment of the exchange with our number system. This would be turned in to the campaign and entered into the campaign data base for various follow ups.

☐ Develop a friendly, open, yet professional greeting. (This depends on the time of day, neighborhood etc.) Just be natural and easy.

At the door

☐ Determine the door that is most often used.

☐ Step back from the door after you knock.

☐ Close any storm or screen door, listening for the click of the latch. This will keep family pets, toddlers, or adults with dementia from making an unexpected or unwelcome exit.

☐ Know what you will do if people invite you in. I played it by ear—it depended on the hour, the weather, and the person. Sometimes I declined.

☐ Know what you will do if someone shuts the door in your face; smile.

☐ Notice political material for you or your opponent in a yard, garage, or window.

What to bring along

☐ Water and food (consider leaving a small cooler in your vehicle, parked in a central yet out-of-the-way location.)

☐ Change of shirt and shoes (you can also leave these in your vehicle for a quick change.)

☐ Biscuits for interested canines.

☐ Campaign literature.

☐ A buddy (try not to door-knock alone. A companion can lend assistance and moral support, and ensure safety.)

☐ Leave literature where it will be safe, not get wet, or blow away. It is illegal to place campaign literature in mailboxes.

What to wear

☐ Good, supportive shoes.

☐ Comfortable clothes that look professional and don't show dirt and sweat (I found sticking to darker, neutral colors with a white or light blue shirt or blouse was best.)

☐ A hat to keep off the sun.

☐ Clothes appropriate for the weather, perhaps in light layers.

☐ Leave the sunglasses behind so you can make good eye contact.

How to identify yourself

- ☐ Wear a campaign button.

- ☐ Put a big bumper sticker on the back of your clipboard.

- ☐ Have your campaign literature handy, even if it's just your résumé.

- ☐ Hand out your brochure, information sheet, or other materials personally so people connect the materials with you. Hold it so the wording faces outward and it is easy for people to read.

- ☐ Avoid knocking on doors during an important sporting event or when most of the neighborhood is at church or a local event.

- ☐ Choose a safe, preferably shady spot to leave your vehicle. You might choose a parking space in the middle of your route so you can return easily for food, water, and clothing changes.

- ☐ Cultivate opportunities to post a yard sign, have a coffee hour, other volunteering. Remember, have your campaign follow up within 24 hours.

Be mindful that you are door-knocking to meet people. You are also approaching them in their most sacred of spaces: their home. They do not expect you. You are not invited. They might be busy, asleep, or, at the very least, surprised to see you. Let them collect themselves and adjust to your visit. Step back and allow a minimum of 18 inches of polite distance. Establish eye contact and allow them the opportunity to speak first. If you see a newspaper lying on the walkway or porch, pick it up and pass it to them. I did not touch the mail, unless they asked me to do so. People are justifiably cautious about their mail.

Approach the various types of housing in your community with common sense and respect. Gated communities or condominium developments might have strict rules against campaigning and door-knocking on site, which you will need to follow. Some neighborhoods require you to get permission from the homeowners' association before you door-knock, and they might refuse. Large apartment buildings might have security. You have to work within the strictures of your community—and remember that knocking on doors isn't your only option. Do it where it works. Reach voters in other types of housing with direct mail, email, telephone calls, social media and other efforts.

Keeping Your Mission in Mind

The secret to getting ahead is getting started.

—MARK TWAIN

Keep your interactions with people positive. Sometimes they will have questions they want you to answer. Sometimes they will want to tell you their own story. They might make a connection with you. Once, when I was door-knocking, a man looked at me and asked, "Are you Dr. Walsh's daughter?" When I said yes, he told me the story of how my father used to pay for prescriptions at the pharmacy for his patients who couldn't afford their medicine. I never knew about this until he told me. He connected with me because he had fond memories of my father. You never know what you might learn when you knock on someone's door.

Standouts or visibilities get your name out and help people recognize you as a candidate. Find out where the people congregate in your neighborhood or district, and when they will be there. It might be a coffee shop, supermarket, gas station, convenience store, transfer station, football game, beach, factory, train station, or golf course. Gather together a merry band of volunteers, put on shoes that are kind to your feet, grab your campaign signs, and go where the people are.

Who's That Standing on the Corner?

In my district, one of the most popular places for candidate standouts is a large rotary, or traffic circle, that gets quite congested with commuters.

When does rush hour traffic pick up where you live? Decide where you will be most visible to the most people, and stand there at that time. I was out on "Holy Name Rotary," standing on a rubber mat to support my hardworking feet, by 6:30 a.m. many mornings during the campaign. We rotated locations to reach as many voters as possible.

A successful standout takes some planning. My sister Madeleine organized my first standouts, and that became one of the most important jobs in our campaign. She engaged the volunteers, chose the locations, determined the schedule, telephoned the volunteers every evening before the next day's standout, and oversaw every detail. Madeleine developed the standout process into a fun, effective political art form. She celebrated volunteer involvement. Madeleine always had her eye out for possible volunteers, and would recruit and cultivate them for Election Day assignments while they fulfilled the regular standout duties.

If you have a large area to cover, you need 15 to 20 people for standouts. For less square footage, you can get away with eight to 10. Bring plenty of sunscreen, both for yourself and your volunteers, as well as lots of water, and consider having goodies or snacks available in the van or truck where people drop off their signs at the end of the session.

Your volunteers should stand an even distance apart. They can dress casually and comfortably, but should look neat and tasteful. There should be no gum chewing, to-go cup drinking, eating, smoking, sitting down, or texting, or fiddling with cell phones during the visibility. The job of each and every volunteer, and you, is to connect with the voters who are driving by. You want to be visible without creating a traffic hazard. Never interfere with driver visibility or block access. Clean up after your standout, and ensure that no debris or litter is left behind.

Campaign standout with Aunt Christina and other friends and supporters

Of course, everyone holds a sign, smiles, waves, and engages the voter—and always has volunteer cards on hand. It might seem simple, but don't discount the critical messaging that is going on while you stand out there on the corner. Your signs should be visible, legible, clean, and in good condition. Your goal, and the goal of the volunteers who stand with you, is to focus on every voter who passes with energy and impact.

Enlist the help of someone with a van or truck to transport the signs. You'll be surprised by the deep relationship some of your regular standout volunteers develop with their signs. They want to decorate the handles, wrap duct tape around them, and take them home. That's fine, as long as they stay in good condition and are there when you need them.

Learn to love visibilities, because as Election Day draws nearer, you'll be standing out on that corner a lot more frequently. In the early days of my campaign, we did maybe one standout every week or two. By the time the election was upon us, my team and I were out there twice daily, during the morning and afternoon commutes, and once on Saturday.

Go Where the People Are

Greeting people in public places at busy times can help build buzz around your campaign, get your name out, and reinforce your personal brand. It is free. You simply have to go where people congregate in your neighborhood or town.

Most likely you can scope out the most congested areas close to where you live. But the election you are running for might encompass other towns and communities outside your zone. Enlist the help of your volunteers to make lists of the places where people gather, and know what times and days of the week these locations are busiest.

In Front of the Crowd, but Out of the Way

Greeting people in public places takes a little finesse. You want to be visible, but you don't want to get in people's way. You want people to see your face and know what you are running for. However, unlike door-knocking, this is not a targeted effort. You don't know if these people are registered to vote or, if they are voters, if they are inclined to vote for you. You are there to get some visibility in the community at large.

When I was campaigning, I might have chosen a coffee shop where lots of people stopped on their morning commute. You might choose the high school football field before the Friday night game, a local fair or festival, or a commuter train station at rush hour. Get there early. Buy something to support the local business if you can. If appropriate, let the people working there know you'll be outside, and assure them you won't be in the way.

Be prepared. Some business owners might oppose your standing outside their establishment. Let them know you'll remain on the public sidewalk, and that you will not infringe on their business or distract their customers. If you're on private property, you will want to seek the approval of the owners and leave quietly if they oppose your presence. Sometimes the owners become supporters and allow you to place a sign in their window, or host a coffee hour in their home or business. Sometimes they will send an email, write a letter or send "dear friend" cards to voters for you.

Then, get to work. Greet people with a smile and high energy. Introduce yourself by name, and say what you are running for. Give them your campaign literature, and leave them with a positive, friendly impression. Be upbeat and visible, but stay to the sidelines and be careful not to make anyone's day more difficult. It is always best to have a volunteer from the local area join you. Find ways you can make those all-important personal connections.

Only have an hour or two, not enough time to set up door-knocking or a formal standout? Hold an informal standout. One of these local appearances can easily be executed, because they don't take much preparation or time. Even an hour outside a crowded store is time well spent to meet a few hundred people with little effort on your part. All you have to do is show up, smile, and be courteous. Don't forget to bring along some volunteer cards and literature for people who offer to support you.

Connecting with Senior Voters

Seniors are a vital part of the political conversation, and older people are often the ones who show up to the polls most reliably. They are experienced. They are aware of the importance of government. They also employ sharp radar that makes them aware of when elected officials are inauthentic. They care about issues that concern their children and grandchildren, as well as the policies and decisions that affect their own lives.

Senior adults also often have lower or fixed incomes. They have more needs than the younger population in terms of housing, transportation, and healthcare. Many seniors today are helping to raise their grandchildren, or taking care of their own aging parents, and they can have a lot of worries and concerns. You're going to hear a lot of questions and information at events with senior attendees, some of which might be brand new to you. Write them down, or have a helper/volunteer do it for you. Then research those issues, learn all you can, and get back to the questioner with an answer or an explanation. This isn't about making empty promises or false reassurances, but about getting to the root of the issues affecting seniors and taking their concerns seriously.

Campaigning with senior voters

When I ran and served, I enjoyed older people. I came to appreciate their enthusiasm and energy level. Older adults arrived at events early, participated fully, and also expected a high level of participation and courtesy from me. The senior events I attended were social affairs, and those who came truly wanted to get to know me, to see I was sincerely interested in their concerns. I approached senior voters and, later, my older constituents, with a visceral connection to what they did for this country.

Those who came before us did their jobs as citizens. Everything we enjoy today is the fruit of the labor of generations who came before us. I look at my parents' generation as an unbroken continuation of that chain of freedom and justice begun by the early colonists and patriots. They were informed and they took risks. Whether it was getting drafted or volunteering for military engagement, growing new businesses, breaking down boundaries and integrating our schools, or creating the infrastructure that runs our world, we have a lot to thank them for.

As you interact with seniors on the campaign trail, keep these four points in mind:

- Get a head start. Arrive early so you will be there to interact with seniors who are always among the first to arrive.

- Listen and learn. It will often be through experienced voters that you learn the systems at play in your area—housing, transportation, healthcare, taxes, assisted living, etc.

- View requests for information from seniors as a gateway to examining the status quo to discover what works and what needs improvement.

- Foster connections. Seniors are often amazing volunteers and generators of word-of-mouth support. Those who live in assisted-living communities or senior housing developments have a close community of people at hand to draw from.

Attending Veterans' Events

As I campaigned and held office, I was very aware that I was not a veteran, and that I was a woman—facts that often set me somewhat apart at events for military veterans. However, my father was a combat veteran, and my four older brothers and sister had served in the military, as had my grandfather. I remembered very well when the mail came and my brothers were activated to serve in the Vietnam Era conflict. I was quite aware of the role the military played in creating America, and I brought that gratitude and awareness to veterans' events.

I was mindful that the veterans I served were in a special category because of their service and sacrifice. Even though I was not in that special category myself, they knew I appreciated their service deeply. During my tenure in office, I successfully shepherded initiatives in support of veterans. At this writing, I am proud to say that my home state of Massachusetts has the most comprehensive state support for veterans in America.

As you run for office, find ways to increase your knowledge about the veterans' community and its concerns. If there is a VFW, American Legion, or other veterans' organization active in your area, find out how you can attend their events or help out. If you are not a veteran yourself, that is okay, as long as you approach veterans' groups with a sincere commitment and sensitivity to their sacrifice and significance.

If you're looking for an issue to champion as a candidate, I can think of nothing more important than advocating for the care of our veterans. At the time this book was being written, America was still engaged in the longest war in our history, Afghanistan, while another long-running conflict, Iraq, had only recently ended. Today, we know far more about the devastating physical, emotional, and psychological effects of serving in combat than we did when my father championed the post-combat care of World War II and Korean War veterans. Thankfully, as a nation we have matured in our approach to those who have served. Supporting our veterans is a truly nonpartisan issue. Today, both those who support and those who oppose military action are united in their support of those who served their country.

Showing Up for Parades

Candidates work very hard on holidays. They make speeches, attend events, and, possibly, march in parades. Parades are important to communities, and they are also a good opportunity for you to be seen by, and connect with, people.

When you are part of a parade, keep the occasion in mind. What the parade is marking governs how you dress, what you say, and how you conduct yourself.

How you travel the parade route is often dictated by the customs of the community where the event is held. Candidates often travel in, or walk beside, a decorated vehicle. In some communities, however, you might ride a golf cart, cruise the parade route in a convertible, or even ride a horse.

However you choose to get from point A to point B, make the occasion and the hosting community your focus. Walk with volunteers from the neighborhood so people lining the route will recognize their friends and family among your supporters and enjoy that sense of connection and fellowship.

Marching in a community parade with friends and supporters

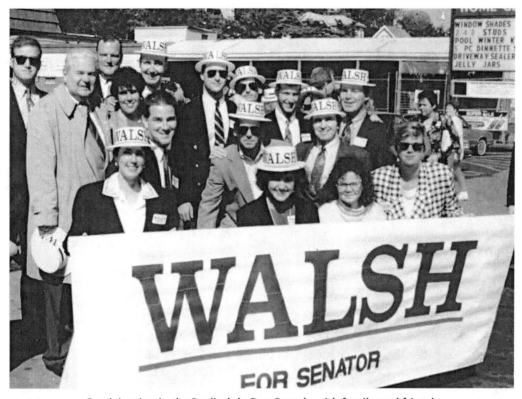

Participating in the Roslindale Day Parade with family and friends

Make parade participation as comfortable and pleasant as possible for the supporters who turned up to help you. Remember to thank them for giving up their own holiday to help you, and provide refreshments so they can refuel after marching.

Smile! You are most likely being observed and perhaps filmed by local cable stations and other local media. Parades are your chance to be seen and recognized by thousands of people at a single event.

Be Your Best Candidate: Checklist ☑

Optimize each campaign opportunity:

At large events (10 or more people at a table)

☐ Have a sense of how many people are present in the room and how many tables there are. Commit to greeting the people at each and every table.

☐ Approach each table slowly. Make eye contact. Smile.

☐ Shake hands when possible and have a campaign helper with you, but standing a little back from you and the table.

☐ Keep your volunteer cards handy, and say something like this: "Hello, I am (name). I wanted to come over and meet you. I am running for (office) and would appreciate your consideration. Enjoy the evening, and thank you."

☐ Keep moving. You will meet and get to know as many people as possible.

☐ If people don't want to be engaged, recognize that and move on.

☐ Tailor your interaction based on what you observe when you approach.

At funerals

☐ Are you present as a mourner or because someone close to the deceased (or the deceased) is prominent in the community?

☐ Be aware and act accordingly. If you weren't close with the deceased or their loved ones, take a seat in the rear of the venue.

☐ Don't wear campaign buttons.

☐ Don't park out front in spaces reserved for the family or other mourners.

☐ Ask yourself: How do I support these people in this experience?

Our first campaign truck with homemade sign

At sporting events

- ☐ Don't compete with the event or interfere with the fans.

- ☐ Be sensitive to families who are enjoying time together, who may have paid a lot for this outing, and who might not want to be bothered.

- ☐ Make eye contact. Smile. Shake hands when possible.

- ☐ Remember your manners and see your presence at the event through the eyes of the attendees.

At train stations

☐ Map out exits and entrances and make sure you are not impeding anyone's path or commute. Have plenty of helpers to hold signs.

☐ Offer literature (facing outward), but don't force it on people.

☐ Shake hands when possible and have volunteer cards available.

☐ Be sensitive to train schedules and the fact that people have somewhere to be.

☐ As always, clean up any campaign materials or debris.

Reach Out with Phone Banks

Whatever office you decide to run for, you will have a better chance of winning if you reach out to voters via every channel available to you. In a typical day on the campaign trail, you might stand out in a public place greeting voters, knock on doors to meet them face-to-face, and mobilize volunteers to call them from a phone bank.

A phone bank usually consists of three or more lines at a convenient location, often a local business such as a real estate, insurance, or law office that has closed for the day. Inquire about a donation of telephone lines; four or five lines are all you need to have a productive phone bank session. Small business owners who want to support you but are busy running their enterprises are often willing to offer phone lines and space to your team for a few hours. Take them up on it. You'll soon have telephones ringing all over town.

Phone banks are most effective in the evenings, so plan them for around 6:00 to 9:00 p.m. Appoint a volunteer to act as "head of phone banks" so someone is in charge of securing a place to make calls from, signing up volunteers to staff the phone bank, and organizing the sessions. Vin Buchanan ran the phone banks for my campaigns, with the help of many others. Vin did this in the evening and on weekends, while working full-time in the private sector. Sometimes he door-knocked with me, and we would catch up on the phone-bank operation as we walked between houses. I would learn about the volunteers, and he would hear from the voters as we knocked on their doors.

Vin would call me at home late in the evening to give me regular updates on the phone-bank progress and status. For example, he would tell me what the voters were feeling, their criticisms, and their comments about me. These conversations were very instructive. We were disciplined and never got too excited or too disappointed with the phone bank results on any given night.

Vin would also let me know what he needed during these calls in order to make the phone banks a success. If he required more volunteers, I would carry that message to the right people in our campaign or get on the phone myself to someone I thought might want to contribute in this way. We always looked for a good fit between a volunteer and the particular project to be done, especially if it was an ongoing job, like phone banking. It had to be natural or it would not work and would not last.

We had constant cross-fertilization in our campaign. We were always aware of the interconnectedness of each facet of the campaign. Being Irish, I would think about a prism of a Waterford crystal: one prism with many sides, each capturing the light to contribute to the brilliant beauty of the whole.

During my campaigns, phone banks served two purposes. First, if I'd been door-knocking in an area, we would follow up with telephone calls to that neighborhood. We would ask if they knew about the current race for state representative, ask them to consider me, and find out if we could get them any information. The main purpose of these calls was to make and reinforce contact with the voter and to send information.

Second, we'd make telephone calls for positive voter identification. Ask the people on your list if they are going to vote in the upcoming election and for whom, and keep track of the ones who say they are going to vote for you. Voter ID is important, because you have to keep building those numbers. Once again, you don't have to win *every* vote, just *enough* votes. The more accurate your estimates, the more confidence you can have in your campaign efforts as Election Day gets closer.

If you've been active in your community, you may have done similar duties in the past. Even if you have never participated in a formal phone bank, you might have been on a telephone tree for carpooling. You made fundraising calls for your child's school or a charity. You place cold calls to gain new customers for your business. You can draw on those same skills now as you build your voter base.

Think of Your Volunteers

Phone banks can be intimidating. When people volunteer to staff them, have your phone bank captain call them to follow up and identify the location and time that works best for them. Hold telephone bank training at your campaign headquarters or at the phone bank location before the session starts. Prepare a solid script, let people know how many calls they are expected to make, and give them a chance to practice. Also, discuss what people should do if they can't reach someone or if they get voicemail. Your goal is to have as much live contact as possible with voters. Volunteers will need to double and triple back to people they could not reach the first time around.

Here I Am, Again

You can never be too visible when you are campaigning. I firmly believe races are won and lost at all levels because one candidate was more "out there" and recognizable than another. The voters in your district need to see you, and keep seeing you. They don't just see you once, when you knocked on their door or stood out on the corner at rush hour. They see you everywhere, over and over again, day after day. This isn't just about visibility. It's about commitment, and hard work. When your voters see you out there, in places that are familiar to them, smiling, day after day, it makes them think about how hard you will work for them when you win. All this knocking, standing, waving, and greeting will be perceived in a positive way. That is what you want, and that is how you win.

Will They Vote for You?

As you go about your dedicated campaigning efforts in your community, you'll be constantly tabulating and readjusting your voter counts. It is useful to put a system in place to gauge how likely someone you meet while door-knocking, calling during a phone bank session, or interacting with at another event will be to vote for you. As you get more exposure among your constituents and begin to reap all those cross-pollination efforts, a simple system will enable you to chart your progress.

I used my own numbering system to predict how likely I was to receive a vote from a person I met at a coffee hour or elsewhere on the campaign trail. The numbers ran from one to four:

1. They are going to vote for me.

2. They are leaning toward voting for me.

3. They are undecided.

4. They will not vote for me.

Surprisingly, I was pretty spot-on with my predictions. Even in my the first campaign the number of votes I earned on Election Day was quite close to the number my campaign arrived at when we added together all those 2's and 1's.

This isn't a scientific process—and believe me, there will be long stretches of time when you feel as though you have no idea how you are actually doing in the race. But there is comfort in numbers.

Nothing is for certain. You can never breathe a sigh of relief, sit back, and say, "I have enough votes." People change their minds. They get sick and don't make it to the polls. They don't register to vote in time. They don't tell you whom they are really going to vote for. Ballots are secret, and you'll never truly know which of the people who said they'd vote for you actually did so.

That's why it is so important for you and your campaign to keep up with the coffee hours, door-knocking, campaign events, speaking opportunities of all stripes, and to follow up via telephone and emails. After you have been on the campaign trail for a while, you do begin to see the same people repeatedly. You see them at a ball game, then the train station; they may have come to a coffee hour at their neighbor's home, or maybe you knocked on their door, then they drive by your standout. Soon you'll hear, "You are everywhere!" Your neighbors get excited and begin to realize how much you aim to serve. This enthusiasm signals that your personal connections are deepening. Your base is growing as well.

Every campaign effort you make in the community cross-pollinates to strengthen efforts across your campaign. Your door-knocking and community appearances will directly translate to a higher number of positive voter IDs from people called by your phone bank. Your weekly meetings with your team will reinforce what you found out during the past week, and set new goals. All the while, you're getting your people in place for Election Day. Every effort builds on the one before, and sets up those to come. Follow these guidelines and on Election Day you will likely have a good idea of how many votes you can expect to receive.

Your community campaigning efforts are your windows into relationship building and campaign development, which ultimately will put more 2s and 1s on your list. In many ways, campaigning is evangelical. Those who are converted to your cause turn around and tell their friends. You, your volunteers, close friends, and family should have blank volunteer cards on hand at all times. Success is when every volunteer signs up one new person a day. That's how your campaign system is built: person-by-person, little by little, day by day, until you win.

It's important to note that whether you are campaigning for yourself or for someone you believe in, whether it's a local race or a presidential race, these same campaign strategies apply. In 2006, Deval Patrick was a relative unknown running for governor of Massachusetts. I felt he would bring positive change and reform to state government. So I campaigned hard for him, building his field organization and introducing him at our state convention, even as I was running in a contested reelection myself. We both won.

As a candidate, I campaigned and worked for all voters: Democrats, Republicans, and un-enrolled, people who did not vote and people who could not vote. On election night, I won so-called Republican voting towns, even though I was a registered Democrat. In 2008, I campaigned vigorously for Barack Obama in the great state of New Hampshire, first knocking on doors and ultimately managing a staging area, in Goffstown, during the general election. He won, too. And so can you.

Taking a Snapshot of Voter Opinions

All my life I have tried to pluck a thistle and plant a flower wherever the flower would grow in thought and mind.

—ABRAHAM LINCOLN

From time to time during your campaign, you will find yourself asking, "How am I doing?" Campaigning probably isn't your full-time job. You might be continuing to go to work every day, taking care of your family, and maintaining your home while you run for office. When I first ran for state representative, I continued to practice law and teach. Eventually, I did have to give up my "day job" in order to devote myself full-time to my campaign efforts. But for a long time I was campaigning on the side, and every spare moment I had was devoted to that effort.

For all of the door-knocking, coffee hours, meet-and-greets, fundraising events, phone banks and standouts, you still might not have a clear idea of where you stand with the voters in your district, or how you are measuring up against your opponents. That's where polling comes in.

Polls are a snapshot, a single image of voter opinions at a particular moment in time. They can be a valuable measurement of your progress, but it's important to keep in mind that the numbers can shift quickly. A poll taken during the early days of your campaign will tell one story, while a second poll near the end of the election can say something else entirely.

It can help to think of polling as an x-ray: You only get the information you need to take the action if they are taken of the affected body part at the right time.

Understand What Polling Can Do

Polling is not useful or necessary in every election. You may not use polling when you run for office this time. But you may need it, for example, when you decide to run for a higher position. In any case, it's important to understand what polls show, and what they don't. Polling can be an incredibly helpful tool you can use to fine-tune your strategy as Election Day approaches. It also can be misleading and used for negative purposes.

What a poll tells you depends on when it is taken, the quality of the questions, and the number of people polled. Take polling in context, and decide ahead of time what you plan to do with the information. You see a lot of polls cited in the media. Keep in mind, the results are often reported in a certain light, with some numbers highlighted while others are left out. Poll results can be interpreted in many ways, making the numbers appear to support a certain point of view. However, the actual hard numbers the pollster gives you do not lie. It's up to you to decide what you will do with that information.

If you poll the voters in your district and don't receive the results you hoped for, see it as constructive criticism. Even negative polling results can help push you forward, because they will reveal areas in which you may be weak and give you the opportunity to grow and make adjustments.

What Polling Can Show You

Polls not only measure how you are faring in your race, they can also reveal how people feel about you personally and how likely they are to vote for you. There are commonly four parts to a pre-election poll:

Favorability

To gauge your favorability rating, a pollster will ask a list of people whether their opinion of you as a candidate is generally favorable, unfavorable, or if they have never heard of you. This is considered a "soft" line of questioning, and mainly shows how well liked you are among people in your district.

Ballot test

Next, the polling expert might give the respondent two choices, and ask them whom they would vote for. They might answer candidate A, candidate B, or undecided. This line of questioning measures electability, which differs from favorability. A poll respondent might rate your favorability high but go on to say they plan to vote for your opposition, perhaps because they don't think you're qualified or sufficiently experienced.

Issues

These questions can be closed-ended. For example, a poll might ask whether a voter is concerned about jobs, education, or the economy. The issue section of a poll may also be open-ended and invite more varied responses that allow people to talk about the specific issues that matter most to them.

Polls that contain this type of questioning are more expensive because they generate results that must then be interpreted to ferret out useful information and meaning. However, when you examine issue questions in relation to other, more straightforward poll questions, they can give you great insight. For example, you might find you are hitting the issues that the people in your district care most deeply about, but you might also discover you aren't winning over undecided voters.

Finding out where you stand with undecided voters is absolute gold when it comes to your campaign strategy. Those undecided people will vote, but they are not yet sure whom they will vote for. You need to learn who those not-yet-committed voters are and discover why they are unsure. If you can find ways to better connect with their concerns and earn their trust, you have a good chance of getting their vote. Polling can help you find out that information, which you can then bring to bear on your entire understanding of what voters need and want. That is information you can use to retool your campaign strategy to connect with voters in a more targeted way and grow the support you need to win and serve.

Demographics

Demographic questions paint a picture of a region based on factors such as age, race, union membership, and gender. Demographic polling can also contain more detail, such as whether respondents have school-age children, their education and income levels, and religious preferences.

A good poll is efficient. A pollster only has a few minutes of a person's time on the phone, and every question counts. Each must be precisely targeted to elicit the most useful information, which you can then employ to inform your campaign strategy. You want a relevant and accurate picture of your candidacy.

When choosing a pollster, look at the campaign reports of prior candidates and observe whom they hired and how much the polling cost. Conduct your search for the right polling expert just as you would hire any other professional: Search online, interview in person or on the telephone, and ask for references. Be comfortable asking the polling organization about costs. Polling is expensive, and you have the right to know how much you will be paying and what that money you will be spending will be used for. Review closely the sampling size, time frames, and confidentiality of the polling results. Be aware of conflict-of-interest concerns as well—you do not want your pollster working for your opponent.

One good website where you can begin your search for a Pollster is http://www.campaignsandelections.com/resources/political-pages/political-category/

Why I Polled

When I ran for the state Senate, pretty much only the people in my state representative district knew me—which amounted to about a quarter of the people in the state Senate district. I took a poll during my campaign for several reasons: I wanted to determine my visibility and my favorability in my current House seat and in the district that I was seeking. Then I wanted to compare the two. I also wanted to know the visibility and favorability of the other candidates who had declared themselves in the Senate race.

I was running against an incumbent state senator, not of my party, and this campaign marked his third run for the seat. The first time he ran, he lost by a close margin. The second time, he was successful. I wanted to use polling to measure his visibility and favorability among the voters, and measure the same factors in the other candidates and myself. It was in my best interest to understand those ratings for all the candidates in the field.

What I Learned

I discovered that in parts of the Senate district that did not overlap my state representative seat, I was nearly invisible. On the other hand, I had very high favorability in areas where people knew who I was. I also learned that among people who lived in the communities that fringed my seat, I had some visibility and also some favorability. In the Senate seat in general, people did not know me. But in the 25 percent of the district where I had served as state representative, I was perceived very favorably.

What did this teach me? That I could grow if I worked hard enough. That the more people who got to know me, the more my favorability would grow as well. This corroborated my instincts that the key to my campaign success was meeting and getting to know as many people as possible.

I Knew I Could Win

Polling sometimes shows the opposite. There are candidates who have high visibility but low favorability. For example, when I ran for state Senate, I had a well-known opponent with very high family name recognition.

My early poll showed the long-time city council candidate to be well known, but also to have low favorability. So even though people knew this opponent, they were not necessarily going to vote for this candidate if there was another choice they liked better. In my heart, I always thought I could win. Those poll results confirmed my instincts. If I worked hard enough, I could win.

I took another poll later in the campaign. It showed I wasn't ahead of the well-known opponent, but I was catching up and was within points of the lead. My visibility had grown, and my favorability was strong. All the door-knocking, the coffee hours, the literature drops I had done were paying off. The poll showed my opponent did not experience the same growth during the period between the first and the second poll. We were building a strong campaign organization, and we worked as hard as possible to continue to grow our campaign.

Managing Your Expectations

Polling can be unsettling and nerve wracking, both while the poll is being taken, and later when you get the results. I was scared to death! What would I find out? Would the results confirm my feelings and instincts, or was I way off base? It's never easy to find out what other people think about you, and polls can play on those feelings of self-doubt quite effectively. You don't know the outcome of a poll before the results arrive, and you can't control it. Accept that, and remember to keep the polling process and the results in perspective. Much like a compass in your pocket will prove a useful tool if you get lost in the woods, a poll can help point you in the right direction. But keep in mind that a poll, like a compass, works best in combination with all your other skills—in this case, instincts and hard work.

Once the poll results arrived, I always felt much calmer. Our campaign was working, and I had secured the information that I was looking for. The polling results had corroborated my instincts. But I wanted to keep my head through the polling process. I knew the polls would reflect what was going on in the minds of the voters, in their households, and in the world around them at the time the questions were asked of them. That information can be enlightening, but it can also be fickle. It does not define you as a candidate or as a person. Approach it with common sense.

Who's in the Know?

Only the pollster and I knew my polling results. I shared them with no one, not even those closest to me on the campaign. I often had polling phone calls conducted from out of state because I didn't want anyone executing the poll to talk to someone who knew me.

I could not tell even one person. There were so many people dedicated to our campaign. There were dozens with whom I was working very closely on the campaign trail. We had sweated, laughed, and cried together. Which one of my dearest supporters would I choose to share those results with, and why? Who would I leave out? By the time we were deep in the campaign, we were like family and I decided that I had certain responsibilities that I had to carry alone in order to preserve the closeness and integrity of our campaign humanity. I kept thinking of my Dad: "Loose lips sink ships." (Incidentally, he never asked about, nor was he given, any polling data.)

I knew we were on the right path, and that we had to keep doing what we were doing, and hopefully, each day we would do it a little better. Sharing the poll results would have created an unfair burden on my closest supporters, and would have put them in an awkward position. So, there was only one copy of my polls, and the results were kept absolutely private.

Some campaigns and some candidates may desire to publish their poll results as a strategic move to advance their campaign or demonstrate an opponent's lack of strength. Each campaign is like a romance: unique. How you employ the results of a poll depends on the circumstances of a particular campaign at a specific time.

Technology Marches On

Part of what goes into creating a successful, efficient poll is carefully choosing the population that will be called and the technology that will reach them best within the context of the poll results you are seeking. The methods people use to communicate are always changing. Good polling takes these changes into account, but also recognizes that some demographic groups tend to adopt the latest communication technology early, while others stick to more traditional methods. Ignoring new technology, such as the latest mobile devices, might skew the poll results and give you misleading information. But focusing exclusively on calling mobile users and ignoring those who continue to rely on landlines would also skew the results. A good pollster knows how to achieve the correct balance that will generate the most reliable results.

A poll should include cell phone users as a percentage of the total number of people polled, but must also take demographic data into consideration. At the time this book was written, people who relied solely on mobile phones were often younger. They also tended to be infrequent voters, or unregistered. So, a poll that included only cell phone users would not necessarily give you accurate data. That poll would not be effective, since you want to focus polling efforts on people who are most likely to vote in the election for the office you are seeking.

In addition, people who get a polling call on their cell phones often say "call me back on my landline" to avoid high costs for the call. Those calls can be considered completed on a landline, even if the initial call was made to a mobile phone.

As tempting as it can be to include the latest technology in polling efforts, it must be done wisely to ensure you're getting the most accurate results. Accuracy isn't just about reaching out to people on the latest communication device—be it a cell phone, smartphone, tablet, or something else entirely. It's how that data is ultimately integrated into the overall poll results and analyzed that matters to your campaign. An effective poll must question the right subset of voters for your particular election, no matter what type of device they are using to communicate. Pollsters should stay up to date with, or ahead of, respondents in terms of new technology, but must also use it in context. Polling is a tool, but should be used in combination with your hard work, instincts, and common sense.

Building Campaign Momentum through Fundraising

Trust yourself. Create the kind of self that you will be happy to live with all your life. Make the most of yourself by fanning the tiny, inner sparks of possibility into flames of achievement.

—GOLDA MEIR

At this point, you might be thinking about how much running a political campaign is likely to cost, and wondering whether you need "seed money" to get started. It's a myth that only candidates who have a lot of money to spend win elections, or that you have to be wealthy to even run for office. But it is true that your campaign will progress more smoothly and your message will reach the voters more easily if you have enough money to communicate.

The costs of your campaign will depend on what office you run for, how many people will vote, and the cost of living in the area where you run. Remember, the cost of living in the same city or state can vary widely, and you may need to be very specific in your campaign spending/contributing search.

For example, a high-profile position in an expensive area of our country with a high voter turnout will usually require a long and expensive campaign. However, if you have strong name recognition because you already hold public office, or if someone with your last name does, or if you were someone recognizable in the community (a local celebrity athlete, a highly visible realtor), then it will very likely be less expensive. Of course, if you seek a low profile, low-voter-participation position such as the elected "animal control officer," you will likely have lower campaign costs.

Throughout my candidacies, I visited both in person and on line the Massachusetts Office of Campaign and Political Finance, (http://www.mass.gov/ocpf), a state agency in Massachusetts. Check your local and state government for a similar agency that regulates and monitors campaign activity.

You may want to visit the Federal Election Commission site, and view the Federal Campaign Finance Law Brochure at http://www.fecgov/pages/brochures/fecfea.shtml, visit the state government sites at http://www.campaignfinance.org/states.html, and explore a site that provides an overview of public funding of campaigns at http://www.ncsl.org.

Gathering the Right Information

Look at what previous candidates spent, if possible. Inform yourself about the campaign-contribution disclosure laws for candidates and office holders in your state. If those laws allow, you will want to find out who gave previous candidates money for the office you seek, the donation amounts, and what their expenditures were. What companies did they use to buy their supplies and materials? What local restaurant regularly delivered food to their headquarters or events? Those businesses most likely supported that candidate. Who donated money? These groups and individuals might want to make a contribution to your campaign as well.

In Massachusetts, I found most of this information at the Office of Campaign Political Finance (OCPF). I could go there in person by visiting the state offices.

It is also accessible online. The corresponding office in your home state will give you the names, addresses, and donation amounts for past campaigns. This will prove useful information as you embark on your own fundraising efforts. You'll get a sense of how much money you can realistically raise, and where it will come from. You might also get some leads on local sources for potential donations and support.

You can also get insight on how much you might expect to spend. I read the campaign finance reports for a wide spectrum of political candidate races: urban, rural, low profile, and state and countywide. I read the contribution and expenditure pages, and became informed about both campaign contributing and campaign spending for various goods and services. I also noted people in my area who donated to political campaigns. All of this information is public record in many jurisdictions. You just have to access it.

These campaign finance reports informed me about the costs, calendar, and process of raising and spending money for a political campaign in my state. I opened a campaign account in accordance with the law, and was blessed to have three most outstanding volunteer campaign treasurers anyone ever elected in America could have had during my service.

Two neighbors and supporters, who served sequentially, served almost twenty years combined: a retired social worker, Ann Colleran, and an Irish immigrant and professional services consultant, Anna Quinn. They did it all. My whole campaign knew they were the bosses, and to run all financial matters through them. They received donations, maintained the bank records, wrote and signed checks to pay vendors and reimbursements, and prepared and submitted the state-required campaign expenditure reports. They stored the campaign records and accessed them when necessary to answer questions from multiple parties. Ann and Anna were incredible for so many years, on and off the campaign trail, and represented the utmost in integrity and professionalism. Being the treasurer is a part-time job, and sometimes more than a full-time job, that comes with a lot of responsibility.

There are campaign software products on the market to support the work of political campaign treasurers. Also, Massachusetts provides training and some support through their state agency to the public and volunteers for report filings, questions, and protocol. Your jurisdiction may, too.

I chose not to sign the campaign checks, although I could have and many candidates do. I preferred to establish an internal check and balance to the daily access to campaign finances. I signed the legally required reports, and took all legal responsibility for the money received and spent on behalf of the campaign.

Everyone knew, you'd better have your receipt for a campaign reimbursement, or be ready to sign an affidavit. But, in all seriousness, I always backed up the decisions of the treasurer, and I followed the same rules as everyone else who worked on my campaign. It was smooth sailing. We avoided any improprieties and maintained the confidence of our constituents and donors. You will want very much to say the same, and you will. Choose your treasurer carefully. The right person will show up when you do.

Making a fundraising and spending plan for your campaign is much like creating your household budget. You determine your financial obligations, look at the deadlines for meeting them, plan how you will raise the money to cover them, and budget for them. For example, you need money to pay for advertising, signage, mailings, and campaign materials. Even raising a small amount of money can lend your campaign more strength and help you earn the votes you need to win.

Making a Fundraising Plan

Look at the calendar, and count back the days and weeks starting with the primary (if you have one) and/or the general election. Nail down how many people live in your district, and how much money will be necessary to reach those that vote. What you need will depend on the office you are running for, how many people you are reaching out to, and your time frame.

Also, be certain to research the campaign finance laws and regulations for your state and district. Make sure you are accepting contributions and reporting them in the required manner, both to avoid problems with the authorities and to run your campaign in an above-board, trustworthy way that will earn the respect of your supporters. I had the political contribution regulations printed on cards, and I kept them on hand in my car or on my person at all times. When I was talking with someone and the question of a contribution came up, the answers were handy and I would share them readily, without breaking stride. Remember that the most powerful and useful words in your vocabulary when it comes to donations are "thank you." They open an answer to a donation question from a supporter, and they close the door after the question has been answered.

Getting Comfortable with the Process

Asking for money might be uncomfortable for you. Remember, your supporters will want to contribute; it is one of the ways they will show their support and appreciation for what you are doing. In turn, let them know that any contribution, in any amount, is welcome. People will want to know how the money is spent, and you must assure them that it will be invested carefully and wisely.

Fundraising isn't a scientific process. Your aim is to come up with simple ways to raise money that incur the lowest overhead costs.

You can also use your own common sense to keep expenses down. All along, I aimed to spend as little money as possible. I packed my lunch. We made our own index/volunteer cards and thank-you notes, and delayed renting a campaign headquarters on our busy main street for as long as possible. We worked out of basements, garages, office, and around kitchen tables throughout the campaigns, even after renting a small headquarters. These measures kept costs down, and allowed people the convenience and flexibility of a decentralized campaign for some activities. Also, keep in mind: the larger your headquarters, the bigger the rent expense.

You also don't have to spend a lot on materials right from the start. My resume prepared on a home computer was my "campaign literature" throughout the campaign. Eventually, we added specific campaign pieces, as the issues and campaign strategy dictated. We used Excel spreadsheets and designed our own simple mail merge and campaign lists from our volunteer cards and sign-up sheets. Certain volunteers entered data, usually from their homes, to be used and accessed by others in the campaign on a regular basis. Included in our databases were volunteer information, "good" voting lists, donations, door-knocking results, phone banking intake, Election Day assignments, and virtually every other campaign activity. A well-organized campaign also helps keep costs to a minimum because you don't waste or duplicate effort.

When fundraising, keep in mind that you aren't chasing money, you are growing connections. If you make real connections, the money will come. Worrying too much about the money can paralyze you intellectually and emotionally, and bring your campaign to a standstill even more quickly than running out of funds. Reach out to your community. Meet people. Tell them you want to serve them. The money will come. People will give you money for the same reasons they will vote for you. The stronger your field organization and the larger your volunteer organization, the more money you will raise. I had more than 2,500 volunteers on my campaigns. They donated to the campaign. If people support you, they will give in all kinds of ways, including financially.

Be Your Best Candidate: Checklist ☑

Fundraisers can take many forms. You can even have fun with them and use your creativity to come up with unique ways to raise funds. Here are some ideas to get you started:

☐ Early breakfasts for business professionals

☐ Weekend pancake breakfasts for families

☐ Family-friendly events, such as an ice-skating, roller-skating, or pool party

☐ Walk-, bike-, or dance-a-thons

☐ Cook-offs or bake-offs

☐ Online donation drives and "parties" held via social media sites

☐ Direct mail letters and phone calls to potential donors

I held an annual Harvest Breakfast at Moseley's in Dedham, with tickets priced at $35 per person. People lined up around the block to get in, and it was one of the most popular events in the community. We offered entertainment and a fabulous breakfast. Besides being a fund-raiser, it was also an event where relationships were sparked and deepened and where people shared in the good feelings generated by a positive, well-run campaign.

Fundraisers don't have to happen in the evening, and they don't have to be big, fancy dinners. You could host early-morning coffee at a small business or home before people head to work, or have an after-work barbecue. Your fundraiser could be as simple as a house party, with a bowl or basket placed in a visible spot for guests to leave envelopes.

Fundraising Guidelines to Follow

Whatever types of fundraisers suit your campaign best, follow these guidelines to ensure they are successful.

Invite your friends, family, neighbors, and volunteers. Ask everyone to bring along one guest. Keep the amount affordable and reasonable. People may be more likely to donate if they didn't spend a lot to attend the event, and you'll get the most results for your efforts when you pack the house.

Please join us in toasting

A Star Senator and True Leader
The Honorable Marian Walsh
**State Senator
and Assistant Majority Leader**

at

Old Colony Cafe
171 Nahatan Street
Norwood MA 02062

Thursday, October 5th
6:00pm to 7:30 pm

Suggested Donation
★ 25   ★ 50   ★ Other

Paid for by The Walsh Committee

Fundraising invitation example

Have help on hand

Enlist a helper to receive checks, and make sure you record the name, home address, email address, phone numbers, including mobile, if possible, and occupation of each donor to satisfy campaign finance laws. Set up a table where people can easily write and submit their checks. But also consider setting up an out-of-the way area with laptops or mobile devices at the ready for your helpers to enter each donor's name, address, donation amount, and other pertinent information on the spot. If something is missing, the guest is still present at the event so information can be clarified or corrected immediately. This saves a lot of time and backtracking later.

Know your crowd

Think about the culture, values, and priorities of the guests you have invited. Make sure the type of fundraiser you are holding, the materials you are presenting, what time of day it is held, the chosen entertainment, and other factors are in line with their needs.

Dress your best

Be attentive to the norms of how people dress for these types of occasions in your community, and strive to reach the highest level of what is normal to wear.

Respect people's time

Show up. Sometimes you should arrive early and greet guests as they come in, and sometimes you should arrive about 30 minutes into the event. It depends on the circumstances and the venue. Remember, the entire experience should feel worthwhile for the people who attend. Respect their time; if they came to your fundraiser, they are already supporters. Fundraisers can be as short as an hour or two, just long enough to receive donations and greet and thank supporters. Events with entertainment may last longer, so make sure people get the chance to enjoy themselves, and one another, as well as contribute. You are building a community. Sometimes the guests are people who have been campaigning hard and it is a welcome break with fellow workers.

The Host Committee

Vasso Anastasiadis ~ Youseff Assaf & Judie Leon
Jimmy & Lucy Bevilacqua ~ Elizabeth Bradley ~ Donna Cabral
Loretta Chmura ~ Bill Fay ~ Ken Hachey ~ George Heos, Esq.
Kevin M. Joyce ~ Victor Leon ~ Vinny Marino
Kathleen McCabe & Beverly Kunze
Marie Mottola-Chalmers ~ Bob & Mary Munger ~ Amy Murtose
Eileen Nee ~ Kim & Kevin O'Connell
Maryann & Richard Ovesen ~ Karen Payne ~ Faith Perry
May Pieroway ~ Rick Quiroga ~ Evelyn Riesenberg
Joanne Rossman ~ Bill Shaevel, Esq. ~ Cathy Slade
Lesia Stanchak ~ Brenda Webster ~ Lucy Williams

Cordially Invites you to an
Summer Evening Reception
for

State Senator Marian Walsh

at

The Birch Street Bistro
26 Birch Street
Roslindale, Massachusetts

Tuesday, June 27, 2006
6:00 PM – 7:30 PM

Suggested Donation: $50, $75, $100

RSVP Envelope Enclosed
Or Contribute Online at www.MarianWalsh.com

Paid for by The Committee to Elect Marian Walsh.   73

Fundraising invitation highlighting host committee names

Have the right materials handy

You want your invitations, signs, and other materials to be legible, clear, and attractive. Also, make sure that your campaign materials suit the culture where you are campaigning. If you live in an area where unions play a significant role, consider getting materials printed in a union shop and placing the union bug on them. If small business owners attend your events, however, materials without a union bug may be preferred. Print materials on recycled paper if eco-friendliness is a concern where you live. Repurpose, re-use, and recycle wherever you can.

Decide ahead of time about alcohol

Depending on the time of day, venue, and attendees, you may decide not to serve alcohol at your event. As a candidate, it's a good idea to abstain from drinking alcohol while on the campaign trail. If someone handed me a drink at an event, I thanked him or her, then quietly and politely handed it off to a helper. I did not have photographs taken with drinks of any kind in my hand, not even coffee cups. They are a distraction, and sometimes a messy and expensive one. The risk is high that you could spill something on yourself or someone else. Light also bounces off glasses and cups, making odd reflections in your photographs.

Rather, let your natural smile and easy posture be the focus of the images taken of you. Strike an easy, relaxed posture that still looks professional, and be sure to avoid the "fig leaf pose" with hands crossed or folded below the waist. Instead, keep your arms relaxed, hands at your sides, and shoulders back.

Show your appreciation

After a fund-raising event, let the host know within 24 hours how much money you raised, and get your thank-you notes out the next day. This is also a great time to enclose one of your volunteer cards because people who have contributed to you financially may want to help out in other ways as well. Don't forget to have volunteer cards come back to your home address, so people know you are the one who sees and handles them.

There are also various electronic tools and technologies that can help you in sending and receiving donations via credit card, online, and mobile devices.

While using these types of devices and technology can make donations more convenient, they also might cost you a lot of money to employ. Look carefully at the costs of electronic tools before you commit to them, and weigh their benefits to your campaign.

Track donations online

If you do use electronic means for fund-raising, consider also using an electronic system to accept payments and keep track of donations. Social media sites and campaign websites can also be suitable platforms for sharing fundraising efforts and publicly sharing how much money you have raised.

How you thank people for their donations, and when, is very important. You're showing your supporters how much you appreciate what they have given. More than that, sending a thank-you is an important way to connect people to your campaign, have them be part of your mission, and remind them to keep the momentum going and vote. Here are a couple of examples of donation follow-up notes I used on my own campaigns.

I preferred an actual thank-you note to an email thank you. It costs more money, but not much more, and I felt it better expressed my gratitude, and allowed for other possible enclosures, when appropriate. It is your preference.

EXAMPLE 1:

Thank you for your generous contribution to my senatorial campaign. It is truly appreciated and will be used wisely.

It is my pleasure and honor to have your support in my reelection efforts. I appreciate your donation.

It would be a big assist if you could contact your family and friends and urge them to vote for me on November 2. We will meet at the Elks Lodge on Spring Street in West Roxbury after the polls close at 8 p.m.

I am here to be of service to you whenever possible.

Gratefully,

Marian

EXAMPLE 2:

Thank you for your generosity to The Walsh Committee. You are now a member of the Maximum for Marian Club, having donated $500 this year to The Walsh Committee.

As a member of the Maximum for Marian Club, you will be receiving complimentary invitations to the events that are planned for the remainder of the year.

Your assistance is invaluable and has allowed us to print literature, signs, and campaign materials and establish a website at www.marianwalsh.com. We are able to rent two campaign headquarters, one in West Roxbury and one in Norwood and lease office equipment and computers for the volunteers to use. We have installed phone lines and Internet service for voter outreach.

As we near Election Day on November 2, I ask that you spread the word and reach out to anyone who could vote for me or help us on the campaign trail, or contribute to The Walsh Committee. All of this can be done online at www.marianwalsh.com.

Two events scheduled at this time are on Monday, September 27 from 5:30 p.m. to 7:30 p.m. at the Old Colonial Café in Norwood and my annual Harvest Breakfast on Sunday, October 31 at 10:00 a.m. at Mosely's in Dedham.

On Election Night after 8:00 p.m., you are invited to watch the returns with us at the Elks Lodge on Spring Street in West Roxbury. We will have our favorite D.J., Dave Solimine; a complimentary buffet, and will watch presidential returns. I hope to see you there.

As always, please let me know if I can be of assistance to you.

Gratefully,

Marian

My St. Patrick's Day Fundraiser

St. Patrick's Day is a big celebration in many parts of America, and in Boston March 17 is a special day. In March, we would host a St. Patrick's Day fundraiser at a local church hall with a large function room and parking lot. We served an Irish dinner buffet and Irish bread. We would hire the best Irish band that we could afford, "The Andy Healy Band." We booked them long in advance. They were quite popular, and we became very friendly. They played for me annually for many, many years. It was a successful and happy tradition, and raised funds for my campaigns.

Around 9:00 pm, I would offer remarks and introduce other elected officials and special guests, as I did at almost all campaign events. Also, I would share some Irish folklore and maybe some personal and political history.

What kinds of fundraising events you choose to host depends on your community, your ancestry and culture, your individual campaign, and your personal preferences. It can also help to seek advice from your friends and supporters. They may have some new, creative fundraising ideas.

Don't let awkwardness surround your efforts. Yes, fundraising is a way to ask for money to give your campaign the legs it needs to get to Election Day. But done properly, it can also be a way to connect with your supporters, forge a bond with them, and give them a key role in your campaign. As you travel the road toward public office, people will give to your cause in many ways. They will volunteer. They will donate spaces for you to use, phone lines, time, energy, and yes, money. Giving and receiving with grace and gratitude will help you create the kind of campaign you want to have, one carried forward by the positive energy of everyone who supports you.

If you feel apprehensive about asking people for money, remember that no person is forced to donate, and that people don't step forward to offer help they aren't prepared to give. Instead, approach fundraising with gratitude, creativity, and even fun, and enjoy the strength it lends your efforts as you work toward a place in public office.

10

The Guidance of the Inner Patriot

Freedom lies in being bold.
—ROBERT FROST

Even before you enter elected office, throughout your time as a candidate, a parade of issues will come before you. Most of these will fall squarely in the center of your comfort zone, and you won't have to think too hard about how to handle them. But others will likely take you on a roller coaster ride. While you're campaigning, you will have to navigate sticky issues, some of which will take you by surprise.

No matter how extensive and careful your preparation, some issues might make you question what you think, know, and believe. You might feel ill equipped to handle them, and you could find yourself pulled in different directions by people with conflicting points of view. The issues themselves, as well as the passion with which people hold to their positions on them, will require you to reach new depths of courage, forthrightness, and understanding.

Progress of the human spirit happens in the rough patches. It is then that we meet the opportunity to advance. Positive change can be cloaked in all kinds of crazy and disruptive disguises.

Campaigning During Controversy

When you reach one of these forks in the road, lean on your own life experience to tell the difference between right and wrong. You can look to your friends, family, and fellow citizens for advice. You can do research, gather facts, and make lists of pros and cons. Ultimately you will find once again the driving and nourishing force that keeps our citizens, neighborhoods, and country moving in a healthy direction. Your decision to run for office invites you to lead from the inner patriot who lives within each of us and who has informed good decisions since our American beginnings.

Taking the Long View

Use times of controversy and debate to deepen your relationship with the voters and connect with why you chose to seek office in the first place. People may stand where they do on a controversy because of intensely personal circumstances and beliefs. Someone who has been out of work for a while and is facing financial difficulty could push for a new big box store to open locally, welcoming the jobs it will bring or the increased competition that will lower prices on consumer goods. Someone else may object to the traffic the store generates during late hours, or prefer that the location be transformed into needed community green space.

It is up to you to navigate these choppy waters and take a longer, larger view. When you strip away the arguments, the fear, and the complex spheres of influence, you start to get at the truth of the matter. Only then can you make a decision that has the best interests of your constituency at heart.

This is your time to bring about sustainable, positive change via the choices you make, the decisions you stand behind, and the ways you execute them. If you want to improve policy, clarify issues, and strengthen the bond between you and the people you will serve, this is your chance. Carpe diem!

To best seize these opportunities and bring about real change, make these promises to yourself and your constituency:

- I will research the issues that come before me.

- I will do my best to know the relevant facts.

- I will seek to understand different points of view.

- I will recognize how these issues affect my constituency, positively and negatively, not just for today, but also over the long term.

Think back to those tenets from the beginning of this book, especially number three: *I will research the relevant facts and opinions and then explain my position.* Tackle the issues at hand one point at a time. Deconstruct them. Understand them. There is no reason to be intimidated by this process. Instead, relish it as a rare and important engagement.

Thinking on Your Feet

Don't worry that you don't know everything there is to know about every issue right now. Those who fought for our rights or for positive change throughout history didn't wake up one morning with a fully formulated plan to change the world. Rosa Parks probably didn't know when she headed to work on December 1, 1955, that on her way home she would refuse to give up her bus seat to a white passenger, setting in motion a new chapter in civil rights history. The early patriots who decided to separate from an oppressive monarchy surely didn't imagine the democracy we enjoy today fully fledged in their minds before they put pens to paper or shouldered their weapons. In controversy, you can often find a compromise. If, when problem solving, you can find a way to compromise, that often reduces discord. People get up every day in ordinary circumstances and go on to do extraordinary things before sunset. That potential lives within you as well. Here are some ways you can harness it:

Show up

Let people know that you realize the problem is important and that you are paying attention. Be disciplined, confident, and visible. You are a change seeker, and a problem solver. That is why you decided to run for public office. If you didn't want to change things you wouldn't be running. Trust yourself, and follow a leadership framework that is both responsible and responsive. People want to know you care and that you are willing to work hard. Often, particularly on the local level, these two qualities are more important to those you serve than whether or not you agree with their position. Remember, controversy often brings an opportunity for solution and compromise.

Learn from your experiences

You have tackled many difficult, perhaps painful, conflicts in your lifetime. You did what was right, and you came up with solutions that you had to work hard to find. Trust yourself.

Look over your shoulder

You might look at how the issue you now face has been handled in the past. You might need to research numbers, facts, and other data. Those larger ideals that inform you as a candidate, such as ethics, social justice, and fairness, are also important in your decision making while campaigning.

Temper your approach

You may find yourself standing in spaces where your opinion differs from the majority of people in the room. Do not walk in with hackles raised. You have worked and lived beside people whose ideologies, personalities, beliefs, and opinions differed from your own many times, and you've worked through it. That's not to say that you must reverse your own position to foster agreement. Know what you believe. Know how you got to that position. Explain yourself well. That's it.

Work with Your Strengths and Weaknesses

If you tend to be more quiet and introspective, you may find it easy to analyze facts, history, and other information. But you may have to work harder at expressing your position clearly and convincingly.

On the other hand, if you enjoy the spotlight and feel comfortable being in charge, you could be swayed by highly charged emotions in a forum where lots of people are weighing in with their opinions and desires. You may need to step off center stage, quiet your own voice, and take time to listen and understand. Then, when it comes time to argue your position, you might find you can persuade people more effectively and voice your views more clearly.

Whatever your strengths, approach your interactions with the issues from a place of calm resolve. Fortify your energy and drive from the people around you and also from the facts. Between those two forces lies the path to a resolution that is best for all.

Be Your Best Candidate: Questions to Ask

- Do you see things through?

- How do you manage when something is difficult, takes longer than you thought it would, and has expected and unexpected obstacles?

- How do you respond to challenges?

The Five Ws Are Your New Best Friends

While serving, I wanted to understand a problem or controversy through an impartial collection of facts. I did not make my decisions or recommendations based only on the current climate or popular sentiments. I wanted to seek the light and lower the heat. I came to learn that when I dug deeper, sometimes all was not as it appeared to be.

Your most powerful tool when gathering and assessing information is one you probably learned in grade school: the Five Ws: Who, What, When, Where, and

Why? Ask and answer these questions often, and return to them every time you're up against a tough problem. They will always lead you along the road to truth and the right information.

The five Ws can help you slice through emotion to get at the factual root of the issue at hand. Matters that appear straightforward at first glance, such as extending a state highway to ease commuter traffic or tearing down an old, dilapidated hockey rink to make room for new development, can be anything but simple once you learn about the community feeling swirling around them. People stand absolutely firm and unmovable on certain issues, and often they are deeply bound to their position for personal reasons. It is up to you to use the five Ws to understand all sides. These five questions will illuminate the right path to take, the one that leads you out of the woods and toward a solution that navigates emotion, partisanship, and personalities to achieve a greater and lasting good.

How the Issues Affect the Vote

Running for and holding office is sometimes like walking a tightrope. You must please your constituents so you can win enough votes to continue to serve, and to do the good work you set out to do. Sometimes, though, being the best public servant involves taking the less-popular viewpoint. When it comes to tough issues, the tightrope sways. On one side, you behave the way the voters expect you to and give them what they think they want, based on the information they have and their personal beliefs. On the other, your inner patriot calls you to follow a more authentic path. What do you do? Do you give the voters the position that they want, or do you give them the decision based on your best judgment? Which do you think better embodies the reasons why they elected— or will elect—you?

There are risks all along this high-wire act. If the voters feel you aren't giving them what they want, they might think you are out of touch. They might decide you aren't hearing what they are saying. The tension stretches between being honest and being popular, being an effective elected official, and being an empty shell ready to only receive and reflect public opinion.

There's a solution that can put you back on firm ground again: Explain yourself. Tell people what you are doing, how you decided to do it, and your reasons why. Learn all you can about the issue at hand, then share what you learn. Invariably, in my experience, doing so improves the entire conversation.

Only you can decide what is worth disagreeing about. There is a time to represent the sentiments of the voters in your district and a time to exercise your best judgment on their behalf, even if it's unpopular. You will know the difference between a matter of great importance and a lower-tier matter.

Often, all that separates you from the right and best decision is a single four-letter word: work. I've talked a lot in this book about positive change, challenging the status quo, and reconnecting with the inner spirit of patriotism and pride. I know those things aren't easy to do. They take a lot of work on the front end. But they often result in less labor down the road.

You make the choice every time you forge ahead on a tough issue. Pay today as you work hard to ride or reshape the waves of opposition to create new and informed popular opinion. Or pay a dearer price tomorrow as you contend with organizations and institutions that disappoint you and public officials who don't represent the best interests of the people.

Leadership that I Learned from a Friend

During my time in office, I learned that truth is sometimes stranger than fiction. I could not make some of this up, nor would I want to.

Every district is different. Every campaign, and every candidate, is unique. My rep district was considered one of the most politically conservative in Massachusetts. It was an urban community with a suburban feel, generally made up of working- and middle-class people, with strong religious roots and a well-established political consciousness.

My good friend Paul McLaughlin, a fellow attorney and a graduate of Boston Latin School and Dartmouth College, grew up in the next neighborhood over from mine, Jamaica Plain, and eventually moved to my neighborhood of West Roxbury and became a homeowner. Paul's family was prestigious and politically active; his father had served as lieutenant governor of Massachusetts.

Paul served as a volunteer and top advisor on my campaigns, and was also in charge of literature drops. Every volunteer involved with literature drops around the community was assigned a neighborhood by Paul and given a precinct map and a pile of literature. We used the buddy system wherever possible, so volunteers rarely walked alone. The literature drop teams also carried volunteer cards, wore campaign buttons, and would aim to meet and engage voters when they dropped the literature at their homes. Literature can be mailed to a mailbox, but not left in one. Under Paul's leadership, we would visit 37,000 homes in a single week.

I sought Paul's counsel when I was considering a run for state rep. He'd had his own unsuccessful run for state representative in a previous year, and he had some valuable advice. He explained he had spent the most money but had come in fourth. Although he felt that his opposition to the death penalty offended voters in our conservative neighborhood, and had become an insurmountable issue in his campaign, he remained deeply committed to his position. I reminded him that I shared his position. Paul was undaunted, and he agreed to help me all that he could.

The death penalty issue came up many times during my campaign for state rep, and I had to explain my position. I thoroughly researched the issue in terms of public policy for and against, its costs, and its history in the United States and Massachusetts.

My position was that first-degree murderers should receive a life sentence without parole. I felt this was the right thing to do. I explained, also, that government-sanctioned murder was an action I could not morally support and therefore, I could not stand in the shoes of the executioner. I could not vote for something that I was unwilling to do.

People listened, responded, criticized, asked questions and so it went, on and on. By the end of the campaign, everyone in my district knew where I stood and why. There was a growing respect for my honesty and clarity. Some people even told me they had not considered the death penalty from all sides before, and had learned something new from me about it. No doubt Paul had planted these seeds in his earlier campaign.

After Paul had successfully helped me win the state rep's seat, he championed my campaign from the House to the state Senate. He had, also become a prominent prosecutor in Boston, and was chief of the Suffolk County Gang Unit. His approach was holistic: hold dangerous criminals accountable for their conduct and support the residents who were held hostage to the bad acts of a few. He envisioned safe neighborhoods in every part of Boston, and it was his then life's work to make them a reality.

In September 1995, Paul joined an informal group dinner at my home. He left early to finish preparing his opening statement for a jury trial the next morning. The defendant in that first-degree murder trial, Jeffry Bly, was a known danger to the city of Boston. Paul dearly wanted a conviction, since he was convinced of Bly's guilt, and knew Bly had gotten off so many times before for other very serious crimes. I drove a short distance to drop off Paul at his old Toyota Tercel, and wished him luck.

A few days later, Paul was assassinated at point-blank range inside that same vehicle as he prepared to drive home from the commuter rail train, shot by someone who had been hiding behind a nearby tree waiting for him. He died before he reached the hospital. After a long investigation and jury trial, Jeffry Bly was convicted of first-degree murder and put in prison for life without parole. I attended the trial, which received national attention.

Today, it still does not seem real that my neighborhood and Paul's beautiful family could have had this horror visit them. It still doesn't seem possible, but it happened. It continues to happen, too many times, to too many people, all across America.

While serving in the district attorney's office, prior to Paul's death, I had been to autopsies and homicide scenes. I accepted attendance at them as an important experience if I wanted to be an effective leader in law enforcement. However, I soon learned that nothing prepares one for the shock and pain felt after a loved one is murdered.

Other horrendous murders followed in the area, including the death of 10-year-old Jeffrey Curley from East Cambridge, who was abducted, killed, sexually abused, and his body was placed in a concrete-lined container and dumped in a river in Maine.[5] Horrific cases like these made headlines nationwide and caused residents of my district to live in fear, confusion, and anger. At the same time, the economy was uncertain, mortgage rates were climbing, and people were anxious about their financial security. Many clamored with a deep-seated fury and vigor for reinstatement of the death penalty in Massachusetts. I viewed that rising tide of opinion as a natural reaction to the dangerous world we were living in.

During this time, I wanted State Representative John Slattery, a Peabody, Massachusetts, Democrat and lawyer, to sit on the Committee on Criminal Justice, which I chaired. I found him to be honest, a hard worker, and open to creating the best public policy for Massachusetts. The then-Speaker of the House, Thomas Finneran, made the committee appointment.

After an exhaustive 10-hour public hearing, the bill to reinstate the death penalty in Massachusetts was discharged with an "ought not to pass" recommendation. It went first to the state Senate, where our committee recommendation was overturned. I debated against the death penalty, and again voted "no." This time was different for me. I was now an expert on the issue. I crawled out of the painful hole Jeffrey Bly created and stared the death penalty monster in the eye. Everything was on the table for me, personally and professionally, and I lost badly, with the Senate overwhelmingly supporting the death penalty, 26-13. The measure moved to the House, and Representative Slattery voted for the death penalty again, just as he had in committee. The death penalty passed the House of Representatives, 81-79.

After that vote, Representative Slattery had second thoughts. He formally requested reconsideration. It was granted, and in the next session the death penalty vote was taken up again.

Representative Slattery changed his mind, even as he was in the fishbowl of a national stage. With his change of heart, the vote stood at 80-80, and the measure failed. Because he switched his vote, there is still no death penalty in Massachusetts. He found the patriot within, and followed it. He was also reelected in his conservative district.[6]

Once the economic climate changed, the crime rate declined, and people started living in a place less defined by fear, many in my state also came to see the inherent problems with administering the death penalty and reexamined its morality. Even more people in Massachusetts today believe our state should not have the death penalty.

I know that Paul McLaughlin's decency and zeal for peace and dignity were manifested in the death penalty debate. I know that he accomplished so much through his power of example.

You will decide where you stand on the issues

What matters is that you do the work it takes to make and lead your way through the tough issue that comes before you. Know where you stand, know why, and know how to explain the way you got there. Stand in a place of calm, informed by the facts, and look past the present moment filled with heated opinions and personal agendas. Envision a future where the decisions made today will bear fruit, and use that vision to muster the courage to do what is right for your future constituents even if it isn't the most popular or expected choice.

Traveling in a Circle

After Paul's murder, I reexamined my stance on the death penalty as a punishment option. I did so involuntarily, silently, and repeatedly. I admit it seemed an alluring option at times. I believe it was the same for everyone who loved Paul. I came to this conclusion: It would have been a tragic irony if Paul's murder had helped reinstate the death penalty in Massachusetts.

We were in a great deal of pain. We also did not know how we were going to win the debate keeping the death penalty out of Massachusetts in such a vitriolic climate.

But we did our best. We used the five Ws.

We collaborated with the informed, courageous leadership of then-Representative John Slattery. And, it all worked out. Answers, solutions, and the victory cavalry all showed up. We accomplished what most thought impossible. We beat back, by one vote, the reinstatement of the death penalty in Massachusetts. Prepare and be ready. Sometimes the impossible happens.

I traveled one, big death penalty circle while chairing the Committee on Criminal Justice. My friend, Paul McLaughlin, led the way.

Talk to People

Our lives begin to end the day we become silent about things that matter.

—MARTIN LUTHER KING, JR.

Sometimes explaining yourself and your position involves informal conversations. At other times, you'll find yourself making a more formal speech. You will employ speeches at many times during your campaign and while you hold office, and those public speaking sessions will serve many purposes, from presenting information to expressing gratitude or asking for support.

So why does the very thought of making a speech strike fear in the hearts of so many? Fear of public speaking ranks high on Americans' lists of fears; people are more afraid of speaking in front of others than they are of flying, terrorists, or even death. (See http://www.answeruniverse.com/what do Americans fear most and http://www.statisticbrain.com/fear-phobia-statistics/)

During my campaigns and years in office, I gave many speeches. You will, too. As you prepare any speech, think about the message you want to convey, the thoughts and ideas that you are striving to express. A good speech is powerful.

It is a way to explain a position, to speak out in gratitude, to voice support or opposition, to call people to action, or even to give those who are unheard the voice they deserve.

Recognize the need for that strong, confident voice, and let it be heard as you campaign. Prepare now to speak up, without fear. There is nothing to be afraid of, only work to be done and a world to make better. Words matter. They are your friends and they will help you in your mission to make the world a better place. Find your words and raise your voice with confidence and conviction. Good things will happen.

Find ways, too, that you can connect with others to practice your public speaking skills and refine your technique. This can be an informal group that gets together periodically to critique and encourage each other or it can be part of a more formal public speaking organization. I found early in my career that my membership in Toastmasters International was worthwhile, helpful, and fun.

Back Again—The Five Ws

That's right, the Five Ws will be right by your side as you prepare to make speeches. Before you make a speech, know the following:

Who will be in the audience?

Who you are speaking to is of prime importance. It informs what you say and how you say it. Tailor your speech to the audience. Remember, it is about them and their needs, not yours. Also, scan the audience as you speak. Are there guests in the front row, people in uniform, or other groups present? You might decide to say a few special words to or about them.

Why am I making this speech?

Speeches have many purposes. You may try to persuade people to take action. You could be explaining your position, or seeking votes, volunteers, or donations. Depending on the occasion, you also could be thanking or praising people, marking a special occasion, or sharing facts. The purpose of your speech should always be at the root of what you say, and every sentence you speak should serve that purpose.

What is my role?

Be aware of the occasion where you are being asked to share your thoughts and ideas. Is it a graduation, a retirement party, an Eagle Scout ceremony, a civic holiday? The occasion itself will inform the content of your speech and determine the tone and your approach.

When...

When you are giving a speech it should be on your calendar with proper lead time for you to prepare, and do well. Knowing what you are doing and entering your speech with a sense of purpose and good preparation will boost your confidence. Whatever the occasion for your speech, try to tie in relevant, current happenings of the world your audience lives in, to connect them to your words and bring them home. For example, whenever I made a Memorial Day speech, I saw my chance to encourage my listeners as patriots. Maybe every listener had not lost someone personally to war, but they had made their own personal sacrifices for loved ones, community, or country. I called them to consciousness and, keeping in mind the memory of those who had gone before, asked if we could better offer ourselves as citizens in today's world.

Be positive, be grateful, speak slowly, and enunciate. Shake the hand of the person who introduced you, and start out by thanking people for allowing you the privilege of being there to speak to them. If you show that you are happy to be speaking to them, your audience will feel happy to be there as well. Look at that—you've already changed the situation, and probably will feel more comfortable. And all you did was smile and say "thank you."

If you do make a mistake in your speech, don't worry. Stay present. Depending on the error and the occasion, you might acknowledge you misspoke or even make light of it. Or you could simply move on. Don't be afraid to pause in speeches, gather your thoughts, and take a breath. Any mistakes you make will likely seem much more significant to you than they do to your audience. They might even help your audience connect with you even more personally, through your shared human fallibility.

Respect your audience and the occasion, and be ready physically, as well as mentally, to make the most of it. Leave your briefcase, purse, and mobile technology behind as you approach the podium. Make sure you have business cards on hand, and are ready to receive the business cards of others following your remarks.

Sometimes the unexpected happens during a speech. Be calm and poised no matter what ensues. If you stumble over your words or lose your place, take a breath and keep going. If someone harasses you from the audience, keep your wits about you, act courteously, and, when appropriate, get back to the topic at hand. Often events are taped and can appear later on television or online, so be mindful of your posture, gestures, and facial expression—and make sure your helpers acquire a copy of the recorded speech for your files.

Keep the length appropriate, and follow closely your topic and purpose, unless there is a good reason not to do so. Speak to people the way you would like to be spoken to. Think about someone you love, who accepts you as you are, and pretend that they are in the audience listening to you. Speak directly to that person and you automatically make your speech more heartfelt, strong, and convincing. When you make a speech, you aren't just standing up and saying words or reading them off a page. You are offering a gift to those who hear you, and inviting them to take part in an important conversation. Even if you are the only one speaking, a good speech can carry the power of many voices behind it.

Words that Leap off the Page and into the World

Write out your speech beforehand, but be prepared to modify it if necessary as you speak. Practice it. Time it to make sure it's not too long. Then fold it up and stow it away. I always had my written words in front of me when I spoke, but I did not read from them. You want to strike a healthy balance between being prepared and being over-rehearsed. I reduced the speech to bullets and phrases, usually on a large index card in large print.

If the speech you're giving is for a large, official event, start thinking about it early. Give yourself at least a month to write it and get ready. Gather and read the research you need for the speech and be aware of current happenings that may affect the speech so you can incorporate them, if appropriate. Alert your staff or helpers and make sure they have copies ready to give out to the press ahead of time if necessary.

If appropriate, smile intermittently as you deliver your speech. Keeping a pleasant, welcoming expression on your face has a positive effect on your audience. It is calming and assuring, and puts everyone at ease—including you.

Remember the nuts and bolts. If you are calling your audience to action on a particular issue, provide materials at the event so they can contact the appropriate people, such as other public officials. If you are thanking people, do so by name whenever feasible. If you are celebrating a holiday, know the history of the holiday and any personal, special meaning it has for your audience and the community in which you are speaking. Done right, speechmaking is yet another opportunity to bring people together, foster understanding, and, perhaps, embrace the desire for change and improvement that led you to seek office in the first place.

Promoting a Point of View

While I was a state senator, a piece of land in West Roxbury located near the VFW Parkway was set to be developed with high-rises for dense housing. This was a rare piece of pristine land previously designated as an "urban wild," a term of environmental protection for a parcel of land within city limits that should be protected due to certain vegetation, wildlife, and other characteristics.

In my speeches, I explained that developing the area was not in the best interests of the community, outlined why, and urged action to preserve it in a form the entire community could enjoy and benefit from. I introduced a bill to preserve the land for open space and recreation. The bill passed, but was vetoed by Governor William Weld. I resubmitted it.

The second time it was introduced, the bill passed again. The governor felt much more favorable about the bill the second time around. I asked Governor Weld (who was not of my political party) to consider signing the bill to protect the land at the site, and he agreed, vacating his corner office for the wooded area to sign the bill. Happily, gratefully, and truthfully, credit was given to Governor Weld for helping to save this wooded area for everyone to enjoy, and we thanked him for giving our neighborhood the balance it needed. You, too, will share credit where credit is due as you campaign and when you win.

The land became Hancock Woods. It is crisscrossed by hiking trails, filled with bird sanctuaries, and has become a haven for scouting events and other outdoor activities in West Roxbury.[7]

Speaking with Purpose in Mind

Speeches about issues like these serve many purposes. When you speak to a candidate or to your fellow officials, you might share facts, explain history, and persuade them to take the right action. When you speak to the public, you reassure them that you are going to do the right thing and that you have their best interests at heart. Speeches can also be your chance to explain what you discovered when you followed the five Ws, and can lead others along the path to understanding more about issues that affect almost everyone.

Finally, you will publicly thank those who supported your efforts, verbally recognizing their contribution.

Remember, many eyes are upon you as you speak, including those of the press. This is an opportunity to build those important bridges, and the words you say can go far. When people hear you speak up and take a stand, they remember it. They might be more likely to help you because of the words you spoke in the past. Speeches, like all your work on the campaign trail and beyond, can lay a strong foundation that will shore up your future efforts and initiatives.

When writing your own speeches, remember to use sensitive, nonjudgmental words that still convey your meaning strongly. A conversational tone will keep your audience engaged, as will short sentences and short paragraphs. Try to only say things that you believe and know to be true. Convey that you respect your listeners, and they will return the favor.

Another Chance to Speak: Debates

Besides making a formal speech, you might also be called upon to debate campaign issues. Let's put it out there right from the start: Candidates don't like debates. Most people running for office will do anything they can to control the debate format, set time limits, and orchestrate the image they project.

Why not take a different approach? Instead of dreading debates, see them as a continuation of the political conversation you have already entered. Debates are simply a way to let the voters see you speak about relevant matters and find out how you respond when questioned about them. They can also fray your nerves, but when you keep your wits about you and apply the same principles you've learned to use in every area of your candidacy, you'll do just fine.

Be Your Best Candidate: Checklist ☑

Prepare for your upcoming debate(s):

☐ Assess your competencies and strengths

☐ Work on areas where you need to be stronger

☐ Research issues of highest concern to voters

☐ Imagine you are speaking directly to the voters you wish to serve

☐ Give the answers you would want to hear as a citizen

☐ Focus on the voters

☐ Give the voters a chance to see who you are and what you think

☐ Be positive, and smile

☐ At the end of the debate, shake hands with your rivals and thank them

Remember the old public speaking adage about putting yourself at ease by picturing the audience in their underwear? I have another piece of advice: Picture everyone in the room as someone who loves and accepts you. Keep that in mind as you answer the questions. You will speak from that place where your true ambitions lie and have no problem saying what the people need and want to hear from you. You will successfully let go of minor annoyances, such as the moderator, the venue, the format, or the time—and you will realize they don't matter. You will also give detractors no reason to criticize you, because your attitude, character, and manner will be genuine and above reproach.

An Unlikely Advocate Explains Herself: Same-Sex Civil Marriage

Speeches can also be a powerful way to share your thought process on an issue and to invite others to share in that journey with you in order to bring about positive change. In the process of writing and delivering such a speech, you might also find your own peace in the face of a difficulty or controversy, as I did from 2004 to 2007 when I became an unlikely voice for gay civil marriage at the Massachusetts Constitutional Convention.

Before I rose to speak, I had traveled a long and arduous road. My district was socially conservative, and the strongest institutional and organizational influence in our community, in my family, and in my own life, was the Catholic Church. Like so many people in my district, I didn't often think about homosexuality. I had certainly had schoolmates, co-workers, and friends who were gay, but I never reconciled my religious traditions with their sexual orientation. I compartmentalized that area of my life intellectually and socially, and for quite a while that worked for me.

Then a requirement of my office turned that neat, compartmentalized world inside out. The Massachusetts Supreme Judicial Court found the right to same-sex civil marriage in the state Constitution, and several groups were working to remove that language and make gay civil marriage unconstitutional. I was a state senator at the time, and I was running for re-election with an opponent who vigorously opposed gay civil marriage.

I came to realize I understood nothing about the issue. I didn't know much about homosexuality, and I didn't know how civil marriage or religious marriage fit into it. I had to peel a lot of onions, layer by layer, to get at the heart of the matter. I used my good friends, the five Ws, again. Again, they saved me.

Building a Bridge to Understanding

I didn't simply sit down and write a speech on the subject. I first examined the issue from all sides and talked to everyone I could. I spoke with gay couples, straight and gay clergy, anti-gay groups, physicians, and psychologists. Every time someone asked to speak with me about this issue, I was open to listening to what they had to say. There was no one I did not meet with. It became clear to everyone that my district was against gay civil marriage. People didn't want me to even consider supporting it, and thousands of calls and emails came into my office.

Finally, I called in my staff and told them I'd made my decision. I felt that our sexual orientation was morally neutral. We must afford gay Americans the same rights as other Americans.

Half my staff cried with joy, and the other half got hives from the stress and shock. My supporters had signed on to help me because they believed I represented the community's interests. I was a candidate for reelection. They hadn't signed on to the gay marriage debate, and they couldn't believe I supported it. Massachusetts was the first legislature to allow gay civil marriage in the United States. Consequently, I became one of the first lawmakers to vote for same sex civil marriage in America.

Late-Night Speech Writing

At the Massachusetts Constitutional Convention on gay marriage, we were in debate for days. The night before the vote, I decided I had to write a speech. I knew if I was going to vote for gay civil marriage the following day, I needed to explain it.

I sat in my family room and wrote. When I finished the speech at 3:00 a.m., my husband generously typed it for me. We slept a couple of hours, then he went off to his work as a judge in the Quincy District Court, and I went to the State House.

I kept asking to be recognized so that I could explain to the Convention and my constituents why I felt that we should not amend the Massachusetts Constitution to eliminate the right to gay civil marriage. The Convention was televised and taped. It felt so very strange to be vying to give a speech and cast a vote that those I loved and represented did not want to hear, and that was painful for me to give. But silence was more painful. I chose to seek light in the hope that it would help extinguish the heat.

The then-Senate president and House speaker opposed gay civil marriage. It took a while before I had the opportunity to speak. Finally, I was recognized. My husband left the bench in Quincy to watch me on a tiny, blurry television in the courthouse. I don't know how I delivered the speech. I had not slept in a very long time. I do not think many people involved in this experience had either. My own mother was uncomfortable with my decision, and my district was not in agreement with my position.

But as I said earlier, a good speech carries the voices of many behind it. When it came time to stand up and speak, I had my five Ws and all my research to lean on. I had my own journey to share. I understood the confusion and opposition in my district and across the state—because *I had gone through the same thing.* I had stood exactly where they did, and now I had the chance to explain how I had come to stand someplace else.

My speech presented a framework for what I had come to believe. I educated. I explained. When it was over, I received a standing ovation. The galleries were full of people. I was advised that my opponent was among them. The place was full of state police. After I was done, I remember feeling exhausted, but peaceful. I felt a sense of dignity, and it felt good. That is the power of speaking the truth. You can't stop the truth. I felt that I did my job.[8]

Following that roll call vote, I learned that I was one of two senators who voted not to amend the Constitution, and to allow same sex marriage to continue in Massachusetts. I was the only state senator who was seeking reelection to support gay civil marriage in the first round of votes at the Constitutional Convention. During the next four-year process required to change the

Massachusetts Constitution, support for gay civil marriage grew. Legislative votes to protect gay civil marriage inched up each year. Ultimately, we secured enough support to maintain the right in the Massachusetts Constitution.

During this four-year public debate, I faced back-to-back anti-gay marriage candidates. Anti-gay marriage groups and organizations targeted me. Yet I won with wide margins (65 percent and 68.8 percent, respectively) in a so-called anti-gay marriage district.[9] At the same time, state representatives in my Senate district opposed gay marriage, and our votes were often contrasted.

I'm sharing this experience because I want every potential candidate, of every political party or ideology, to see that what matters, above all, is to be genuine, work hard, be thoughtful and respectful, listen, and tell the truth. At the heart of every issue, no matter how divisive, are facts. It is those facts that you need to know, and be able to explain and share, in order to lead.

As I write these words, I smile, because the gay marriage debate that was so turbulent and required all of my skill, talent, and time for a few years is now a political yawn in my state. Gay civil marriage is now a "given" in Massachusetts.

Child labor laws, Social Security, minimum wage, women's voting rights—these are all political yawns now. But before the yawns came disruption and tension, speeches and votes that were very difficult for elected officials. Remember that process. It is one that will continue to occur time and again, and it is a vital, beautiful part of our political system. Now is the perfect time to take your place in the continuum, to stir up the pot as those who went before you did. Run. Take up the torch. Be part of the great things that need your involvement and your special talent and dedication.

The Lessons of the Past

Whether it is gay civil marriage, the abolition of slavery, or saving a skating rink, you have the same path to follow. During difficult days of disruption, things often do not appear as they truly are. If they did, we would reach a just and dignified resolution with ease, and there would be no conflicts or tension.

It is an embarrassment today to most residents of this nation that we held black Americans in bondage and considered them property, or that women were seen as unequal to men and prohibited from voting. These issues seem so clear, so obvious to us from our modern viewpoint—and, especially to young people, they seem part of the distant past. It's hard to identify with a mindset that appears so obviously wrong to us now. That these things happened seems incredible.

Sometimes we do not see things as they are in the midst of turbulence. Lots of good people thought women should not vote because they were not mentally capable of deciding whom to vote for. Many did not object to slavery, because they did not view African-Americans as human beings.

Attitudes, opinions, and feelings change. But the facts never do. These injustices were as bad and unacceptable when they happened as they appear to us now. It took those first few people with the courage to object, speak out, and work to bring about social justice to illuminate the facts, and assure the freedoms we now take as a matter of course. We changed, America grew, and the same facts look different to us than they did to Americans just a few generations ago. African-Americans won civil rights, women won the right to vote, and some day soon civil marriage for gay Americans will join that list as a basic right.

We are losing the FEAR: False Evidence Appearing Real. The facts are so important because they are what extinguishes the fear. Base your speeches on facts. Gently inform your candidacy with facts, and you will run and speak from a secure and positive place of respect and understanding.

Fear has many disguises. People justified slavery as a source of the inexpensive labor that drove the Southern economy. People were uncomfortable with women having interests outside the home and less time for their husbands and families.

People in general are often uncomfortable with stepping into the unknown or experiencing something outside their cultural norm.

In the gay civil marriage debate, fear was a prominent and imposing visitor. It lingered behind and around me as I prepared and delivered my speech at the Massachusetts Constitutional Convention. But the more I learned, the more capable and prepared I became to make a rational and moral decision involving the civil rights of my fellow Americans.

As the passage of time caries us further away from the social turbulence and power struggles that surrounded certain issues in our country, we gain insight. We gain the ability to see things as they truly are because we lose the fear. We find comfort and familiarity where we once saw nothing but turbulent, frightening upheaval. What begins as disruptive, even shocking, change eventually becomes the status quo. And we will yawn once again!

Tomorrow's status quo is today's disruption. I am grateful to the five Ws. They bring light, not heat, every time. I did not always have the answers, but by posing the right questions, then seeking truthful answers, even unexpected ones, I always reached a solution. The facts will always work for you, especially when they are integrated with your values, character, and strategy.

(In an appendix at the end of the book you'll find a number of speeches, including the one I gave at the Massachusetts Constitutional Convention on gay marriage.)

Leading with Heart, Mind, and Soul

I believe we are here on the planet Earth to live, grow up
and do what we can to make this world a better place
for all people to enjoy freedom.
—ROSA PARKS

When you walk, jog, or drive around your neighborhood, how do you feel? I remember driving through my district, returning home following late-night sessions, feeling like a parent going in to check on the baby. I knew who lived in the houses and apartment buildings, who owned the businesses, and what they needed, both personally and for the community. I loved that feeling. Running for office will lead you to learn so much about where you live and the people who live there with you. That deep connection is where your courage and determination to be a good leader will come from. You develop your leadership skills from what is best for those you serve, much like a parent is compelled to fight for their child.

Leaders are not born; people are born. Each of us has a leader within, and we lead in our own lives, learning to meet our potential and find happiness. Some of us are better at it than others, but the roots of leadership are within each of us, if we dig deep enough.

Each of us is born into a family, a culture, and a neighborhood. Each of us carries the past and the expectations of those institutions, to some extent, on our shoulders.

Now we realize that some early Americans were people who tapped into their creative and courageous leadership when they broke from an oppressive monarchy and declared their independence. They were able to imagine a new community where people were respected, enjoyed freedom, and shared responsibility.

They gathered together and, at great risk to themselves, wrote down their ideas, values, and hopes. Sometimes they argued. Sometimes they were scared. They perhaps weren't sure what their ideas would look like on paper, or whether their efforts would make any difference in the world. Despite all that, they stayed the course. They responded to and rebutted criticisms and questions from friend and rival alike.

These early Americans summoned the leader within themselves. They had no teachers, no role models, and no safety net. As more people read their ideas and listened to their voices, their words became a clarion call that something beautiful and free was about to arrive, and that it could not be denied. This new place for equality, dignity, and respect was called America. The developers of this new space sought out and built a singular community for freedom, with strength, conviction, and hard work.

Recognize your own value and potential, summon your courage, and step up. Nobody is going to call your number and let you know it's your turn to lead. The impetus to take the helm comes from within. There is awareness, consciousness, and love that already lives inside you. All you have to do is uncover it, and follow where it leads you. Then use that voice and that power to advocate for your community and fellow citizens.

Lean on, and Learn from, the Past

If you doubt the power of your own voice to instigate change or make a difference, I have a story for you. When I first started teaching leadership courses on the university level, I came across the essay "In Politics to Stay: Black Women Leaders and Party Politics in the 1920s," by Evelyn Brooks Higginbotham. The essay describes the role black women in Chicago played in getting out the vote and getting candidates elected between 1900 and 1930.[10]

These women instigated change. Many of them were poor, uneducated, and illiterate. None of them were able to vote themselves. And yet they penetrated the abyss. They made their mark on politics, and it was one that endured. In the wake of the Civil War and World War I, they were not satisfied simply to migrate North in search of a better, freer life. They sought to change the political conversation.

Even before women won the right to vote, these politically active black women were finding ways to make their voices heard. They educated black Americans about voter registration, got them to the polls, and helped them through the process. They questioned candidates about the issues important to them—child labor laws, equality and anti-discrimination, the 19th Amendment. They worked to support those candidates who would best represent their needs, and the needs of their neighbors, in the public square.

Before I'd read this essay, I had never pondered, or even heard of, the role of black women leaders in getting candidates elected in the early decades of the twentieth century. I found it absolutely inspiring and uplifting. These women had no political experience. They had no money or power. And yet they were instrumental in the 1915 election of Oscar DePriest, Chicago's first black alderman, and played a role in electing William Hale Thompson as Chicago mayor that same year.

All this proves that you don't have to be rich, educated, or part of the ruling majority to make a difference. These women were the daughters and granddaughters of slaves. Their fathers and uncles may have served in the

Civil War. They experienced first-hand segregation, violence, and economic oppression in the South. After migrating north, they were still often denied housing, employment, and cultural inclusion.

However, instead of staying silent in the face of economic and social hopelessness, they found ways to break with the past. They channeled their energy into positive actions that could make a difference for themselves and future generations.

What I'm describing here is political involvement at the most nitty-gritty level. Those black women supported Democrats and Republicans, candidates in elections from city alderman all the way up to President of the United States.

If you find yourself disgruntled at the state of affairs in politics and in America today, realize that those feelings are not new, and that you are far from the first to have them. Recognize that avenues are open to you. There are actions you can take. All you have to do is make your way toward them, and keep moving forward.

Leaders Also Live Right Next Door

When I served as a state representative, my district was largely Irish-Catholic, Italian, Lebanese, Greek, and Jewish. My constituents were mostly working-class, with spikes of wealth in certain neighborhoods.

When I ran for state Senate, my district was larger and much more diverse. People who lived in Boston wanted a state senator from the city, while those in the suburbs wanted to vote for a candidate from the suburbs. Many immigrants lived in my district, and I always felt close to that community. Three of my four grandparents were immigrants who came through Ellis Island. Also, while a divinity school student, I had studied religions up close and in depth, both new and established. I felt comfortable with the many ways people expressed their culture, concerns, and spiritual life. The diversity of my constituency both challenged me and brought me great joy.

The new patriots are all around us, and they did not come over on the Mayflower. Perhaps you are a new American citizen, or your parents immigrated here and you are a first-generation American. You are American enough. You can run and win.

What Makes a Leader?

What is a leader? People may define leadership differently, depending on their background, country of origin, and other factors. In America we follow a democratic model, where our leaders work cooperatively with the people to achieve a greater good. In other countries, leadership is hierarchical, with a top-down structure and strict chains of command. Some cultures value leaders who are outspoken and authoritative, while others look to people who have a quieter, more understated style.

Leadership preferences don't just vary from country to country or continent to continent. In your district, you will likely encounter a cross-section of different cultures, ethnic backgrounds, religions, financial profiles, and languages. These differences can define what specific groups look for in a leader, and they are not all the same. It is up to you to understand those needs and work with them. At the same time, know that some traits are universal, understood by all, and available for you to develop and grow so you can be the most effective leader for every person across your constituency.

However, there are certain underlying qualities that make a leader. The Global Leadership and Organizational Behavior Effectiveness (GLOBE) studies reveal that certain positive and negative traits associated with leadership remain constant, even across cultures and nationalities. The basic traits that make someone a leader do not change and live within each of us.

People who are effective leaders are:

• Trustworthy	• Just
• Dependable	• Problem Solvers
• Foresighted	• Decisive
• Encouraging	• Confidence Builders
• Positive	• Motivators
• Honest	• Communicators
• Intelligent	• Planners

Leaders are usually good coordinators, organizers, administrators, and team builders. They often seek to solve problems in ways that enable everyone to win.

Leadership traits also tread a fine line, leading people who have strong personalities to risk displaying qualities that are more negative. Undesirable leadership qualities include being:

• Ruthless	• Uncooperative
• Asocial	• Egocentric
• Dictatorial	• Irritable

One way to ensure you don't drift from positive to negative is to always keep those you serve in the forefront of your mind and consciousness. Think first of the needs and positions of your neighbors and fellow citizens, and make benefitting them your overarching goal.

As you campaign, devise ways to remind yourself of the real reasons why you run. For example, I declined legislative plates on my vehicle, even though they were offered to me time and again. I still do not know why we have them. I'm sure nobody but me noticed that I used my own civilian plates on my vehicle. It was a private little reminder to keep my eye on the ball. It kept me in touch with my positive leadership traits, and helped create a healthier distance from the negative ones.

It doesn't have to be a big thing. It can be some small, personal reminder of your reasons for running and serving. Those reminders can keep your mind focused as you try a new approach, take a risk, or espouse a not-yet popular position in order to bring about positive change. They are individual and personal triggers that will help you stay in touch with what matters. Figure out what they are for you, and keep them handy.

Be Your Best Candidate: Questions to Ask

Circle the qualities that apply to you. Are you

Shy

Friendly

Outgoing

Purposeful

A team leader

A team member

A team builder

What do each of these terms mean to you?

_____

_____

_____

_____

_____

_____

_____

How might these qualities affect your campaign?

_____

_____

_____

_____

_____

_____

_____

A Mother's Leadership and Love

Shortly before I wrote this book, I attended a birthday party for a couple who lived in my district—the husband was turning 90, and the wife 80. Their names are Al and Janet, and they live in my hometown of West Roxbury. Janet is of Lebanese descent, and is very informed, intelligent, and outspoken. She originally campaigned against me, but after I was elected, eventually became one of my supporters and was very active on my behalf during many of my campaigns and my time in office.

One day, Janet called me in distress. Her son had been diagnosed with amyotrophic lateral sclerosis, or ALS. Janet used her intelligence, drive, and motivation to become an expert on the disease and an advocate for her son. She tracked down the most renowned doctor and researcher for ALS in the country, Dr. Robert Brown, who was then working nearby at Massachusetts General Hospital, and she secured him as her son's physician.

I went with Janet to visit Dr. Brown at his research laboratory and learned alongside her all I could about ALS. Janet's greatest desire was to create an ALS registry that would collect data about people suffering from the disease.

She believed fervently that with this registry, doctors like Dr. Brown would get more research dollars, bringing us closer to an ALS cure. She began working the ALS Association of Massachusetts and its Executive Director Rick Arrowood, to advocate for an ALS Registry. This project became her life's work, and it became my part-time job as well.

In 2003, through the efforts of the members and families of the ALS Association of Massachusetts, and the leadership of Rick Arrowood and Janet, our state passed legislation establishing the first ALS registry in the United States. (In 2010, the federal government created a national ALS registry.)[11] Her son attended that combined eightieth and ninetieth birthday party for his parents, with his own young daughter and wife. Without Janet's hard work and leadership, current and future ALS sufferers would have less hope. Instead of giving up, Janet used her head to learn everything there was to know, to find out every possibility and to explore every avenue relentlessly. Then she used her heart to guide her toward solutions and inspire her to push past opposition and difficulty.

When I ran for and won office, I certainly had no idea I'd be involved in passing ALS legislation. Through Janet's motivated, confident, and consistent leadership skills—combined with her love for her son—we brought about positive change. And remember, this was a woman who had originally been my opposition! That's another important thing about being a good leader: You build bridges. As you combine caring, common sense, and an appetite for problem solving, you will happen upon relevant, timely solutions that are grounded in fact and carried forward by a positive, undefeatable attitude. That's leadership, and it resides in you, too.

How a Leader Serves the Public Well

When you are elected, you will serve the public. Each member of that public has an opinion that deserves to be heard and considered. As you run and while you serve, you will have the chance to share ideas and information from your constituents that navigate and sometimes unite differing points of view. This collaborative leadership is the best kind there is. I saw this on many occasions in my time in office. I remember fondly how well Governor Paul Cellucci, who was not of my party, and I worked together on a number of issues.

Remember that first important tenet of running for office from Chapter 1: *You will learn from others.* Great leaders listen as well as speak, and seek to understand the basis for others' positions and beliefs. As a candidate and an elected leader, you can shape, inform, and challenge public opinion. The public can do the same for you. When you truly listen to and strive to understand public opinion, you gain insight into how people think and what they care about. You might find your own views change a bit as a result of that influx of insight and information. That flexibility and willingness to learn will make you a better candidate and elected official, and a stronger leader.

This process isn't always a straight line. Sometimes it can be a little clumsy and convoluted. For example, we may want our candidates to sign a "no new tax" pledge, yet we will vote for an override on our local ballot to raise money for the neighborhood high school our children attend. We may advocate "buying local" and "buying American," but then buy garden hoses made in China and cars made in Sweden.

An effective, caring leader takes all of this in and pays close attention. Listen for what your constituents really want; it may not be what they say they want. A skilled and attentive leader soon realizes that voters want leaders with values and want to trust those whom they elect.

Think of public opinion as a snapshot of a certain moment in time. What you are hearing might be just one person's opinion. What you read might be a single blogger or columnist's viewpoint. Or it could indicate the tip of a larger iceberg. Public opinion is part of the political terrain, and it can help you. Remember, you know more about some things than the voters. That is your job. That is why they want to hire you and place their trust in you to make good decisions. Often, when you offer informed, timely leadership, public opinion follows. That's when good things happen and the status quo begins to shift.

A step closer to bipartisan progress—Democratic legislators join the late Gov. Paul Cellucci (MA-R) as he signs a bill at the Massachusetts State House.

Who Inspires You?

As you explore your leadership skills and develop and deepen them on the campaign trail, consider the people you admire. They can illuminate your path to office and be supportive pillars once you get there.

When I chose to run for office, I was greatly inspired by my congressman, Joseph (Joe) Moakley. I learned so much about how to serve and lead from him, and I aspired to do as good a job serving the public as he did. Eventually, he and I became close and we worked together on many matters that affected our mutual constituents. He passed away while serving in Congress but is remembered for his unparalleled dedication, instincts, and skill. I still miss him. My father, Eleanor Roosevelt, and Mother Teresa were also inspirations to me.

The late Congressman Joe Moakley at the Harvest Breakfast

Who inspires you? This is an important question to explore as you prepare to take on a leadership role. As you get ready to run, think about the people who have made a difference in your life. What qualities and personality traits in them do you particularly admire? Whether they are public figures or people you know personally, role models are beacons to help light your way throughout your campaign and your time in office, as well as in everyday life.

What are the qualities we admire most in those who motivate us to do more, be better, and reach the highest pinnacle of our potential? Our role models are courageous, fair, kind, and truthful. They are steadfast in the face of adversity. They worry more about doing the right thing than about "being right." These are people who blazed the trail, so when the way seems dark, you have only to turn your footsteps in their direction to find your path again.

Think about the different strengths each of your personal role models manifest, and why you feel drawn to them. You might choose an inspirational quote by one of them or even put a picture of one in a prominent place.

These little reminders connect you to the unique spirit and passion you share with others and lighten the load during difficult times. As you keep moving forward on your path to candidacy and office, they will help you take joy in the process and make the journey a delight. They will also help you remember that you are not the first to tread this path or do something difficult but worth doing. Remember, if it is too easy, you are probably not making a difference.

Always look to people within your campaign for inspiration, support, and guidance. In the minds and lives of your role models, your constituents, your family and friends, your neighbors—that is where you will find the reasons why you run.

Know What You Believe

When you consider all those inspiring people who came before you and live around you now, you might notice something. Being a leader doesn't mean you stand up and speak out constantly, or that your voice is louder than everyone else's, or that your opinion counts more. You can be an accomplished leader even if in the beginning you feel anxious talking in front of people, even if you make mistakes or sometimes are not sure how to say what ought to be said.

In fact, those vulnerabilities can help make you an even better leader. They keep you in touch with your humanity, and can forge an unbreakable bond between you and those you hope to serve. You will also gain support when your constituents can see themselves in you. When you seek to serve your community, you become an instrument. Misgivings tend to melt away once you realize it's not about you. You are the facilitator and the motivator.

The Impossible Becomes Possible: The Rink

One of the most challenging and satisfying projects for me was the near closing of a publicly owned skating rink in West Roxbury. While campaigning, I learned that there was about to be a big lock on the door of the rink, because of its state of disrepair. The hours were being scaled back, and it was closed for weeks at a time during the season because the equipment could not handle temperature drops and spikes. The Zamboni wasn't working. The restrooms were out of order. The roof leaked. It had become a political albatross, as well, and the then-governor resisted taking it on as a public works improvement project, even though the hockey parents who ran the rink were seeking state assistance.

Unlike some of my friends, I had never been a "rink rat." My most prominent childhood memory of the place was skating awkwardly around while preteen boys tried to pull off my hat. But as an elected official, I knew we needed to save this rink. It was more than a skating facility; it was an intergenerational community center, an almost-sacred depository of local fun, blood, sweat, and tears. It was a special place where character was developed and lifelong friendships established.

Hockey players at the "New" West Roxbury Rink

In the Boston section of my district there were few neighborhood schools or Thanksgiving football games that rallied the entire neighborhood because of student busing and various city school assignment plans. But hockey championships were an ordinary, expected part of life, and many people were heavily invested in our fabled youth hockey league success.

I invited everyone deeply involved to sit around my family room table after business hours, while my staff and I gathered all the facts and followed the five Ws: What would it cost to fix? Why was it losing money? Who used it? What factors had led to it falling into such disrepair?

I discovered that even though the rink was in West Roxbury, it was also a haven for families who lived in other communities in my district (and outside of my district), including the next neighborhood over, Roslindale. I presented the plight to Pat and Bud Roche, who founded and owned the popular Roche Brothers grocery store, the second largest food store chain in New England.

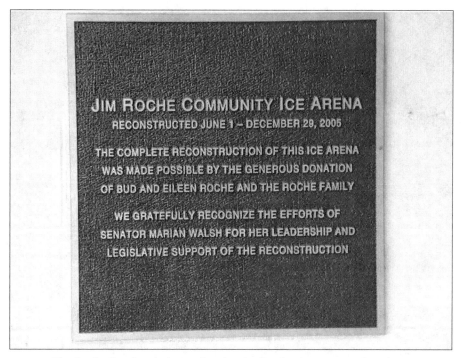

The Roche Brothers' plaque for the Jim Roche Community Ice Arena

My staff and I did our due diligence and learned all we could about rinks, construction, finance, and conservation. The rink was built on the banks of the storied Charles River. Because of environmental laws it could never be built there today, and we could not expand the rink footprint.

We needed to learn the universe of costs for renovation and repair. We had to secure management reforms both inside government and in the community. After meetings with the Roches and many follow-up communications with their legal counsel, various government officials, and constituents, my office drafted legislation.

We proposed a trust fund for capital expenses, an advisory board, and a management plan for concessions, operations, and maintenance. We assured the Roches that the sound fiscal and facility management they sought would be the standard operation procedure for the future, and it was part of the legislation. The Roches donated $2 million, conditioned upon the state contributing $1 million to the rink project. The Legislature and the then-governor Mitt Romney, not of my party, after considerable advocacy and education, supported our legislation without dissent.[12]

Within a year and a half, the community had a state-of-the-art ice rink, and we had created a new model with the bond we forged between private philanthropy and government. I believed deep down that the community deserved a new rink, and also believed that the government had let them down. Today, the rink is safe, clean, beautiful—and profitable.

We did not know what the solution would look like, but we knew we would find one, and we did. We did not ignore the issue or blame others for the demise of the rink. Nor did we give up, and prepare the rink's wake and funeral.

For anyone who may not know Pat and Bud Roche, they are brothers and hail from the Roslindale neighborhood of Boston. They embody the American Dream: From modest beginnings they founded and nurtured the second largest food store chain in New England. Innovation, quality, service and quiet philanthropy are their hallmark. They have been exemplary employers and more comfortable with anonymity than celebrity. The Roche brothers made our new rink possible, and this is just one of countless examples of their generous and loving citizenship.

When you put those universal, intrinsic leadership qualities to work—trustworthiness, problem solving, dependability, and optimism—people see the chance to feel good about their government and their institutions again. You reach solutions that benefit all sides, and give those ideas a chance to survive, thrive, and gain momentum. All that happens when you put your good qualities to use, apply the five Ws, and heed the call to your authentic and unique leadership.

As I explain to my coaching clients, positive leadership qualities are also infectious. They help everyone around you feel good about themselves, about each other, and about their community. Effective leaders don't have to force people to follow them. They don't get support for their ideas because their voice is the loudest or their personality the strongest. Know that by stepping forward, you take the first step toward growing into the leader your community is looking for, and that you can personally become.

Be Your Best Candidate: Questions to Answer

Who inspires you?

List four people who are inspirations in your life

_____

_____

_____

_____

Why do they inspire you?

_____

_____

_____

_____

What words do you live by?

_____

_____

_____

_____

What quotes and wise words do you find inspiring or look to time and again for guidance?

Write down three of your favorite quotes

_____

_____

_____

_____

_____

_____

_____

_____

_____

_____

_____

_____

_____

_____

Faith, Religion, and Politics

Just as a candle cannot burn without fire, men cannot live without a spiritual life.
—SIDDHARTHA GAUTAMA (BUDDHA)

Politics and religion are inextricably connected, although we in America officially separate them and protect and guide that separation with our Constitution and other legal frameworks. Despite this separation, we know and live out daily the seamless melding of religion and politics. The connection between the two is inescapable, from the evolution debate in our public schools to prayer at civic events, from public policy on gay civil marriage and abortion to varying perspectives on global warming.

We realize that our government should neither oppress nor cultivate any particular religion. As a nation, we go even deeper in the weeds of this conversation to make it clear that while people may believe anything they choose, a person may not behave any way they choose while claiming to manifest their religion. Certain behavior is prohibited, even if it might be deemed religious by some, such as human sacrifice or abuse of women and children.

Although church and state are separated in America, it can be difficult to remove faith from the political conversation. Most of us do acknowledge some higher power, some source from where all life emanates, although we may each call it by a different name. Our relationship to that higher power informs our beliefs, instincts, and values, and guides the decisions we make.

The religious organizations and institutions in our communities are often influential. They set forth rules and recommendations that guide their members' positions on issues, and sometimes influence how they vote as well. For these reasons, I think a book about running for office cannot be complete without some discussion of religion and faith, and their relationship to politics.

I do believe that "faith" and "religion" are not necessarily synonymous. I understand faith as referring to a person's spiritual development and mystical core. It is pure and informed by our Creator or Source. I see faith and spiritual development as interchangeable. I view our faith as that vital, enduring, and vibrant connection with one's Creator or Source. For me, this is God. God is love. Love is God. I believe the beginning is love and there is no end, just more love.

Polls show that most Americans do believe in God or some creating Source, and that most Americans pray. That describes faith as I understand it. What I also know is that so-called "nonbelievers" vote and love, and love their country, too.

Many people belong to faith-oriented communities. These are usually called a religious group or church. Many churches and religions have structures, from formal to informal, and often have an organizational hierarchy and a chain of command. Some religions are newly formed, while others are very established.

If a particular religious institution has a large membership among your constituency, you probably need to understand and be aware of its perspective on big issues and its ability to influence the flock—your voters. This information will help you hold more intelligent, sensitive conversations, especially when controversial issues arise.

Your constituents may rely on religious leaders in making decisions. For that reason, the position of religious institutions on matters that straddle the line between politics and personal lives—such as birth control, abortion, sexual orientation and the death penalty—might factor into your campaign. At times, religious beliefs might even interfere or compete with facts you've uncovered as you followed the five Ws. This can create conflict where you are looking for resolution, and generate anger when you need more constructive emotions to come to the fore. Keep your sense of loving and informed service and your path will be clear.

How Spirituality Informs Politics

My spiritual life is very important, and always has been. My parents were faith-filled and lived out the loving example of God each day, quietly and purposefully with joy and gratitude. They belonged to a Catholic Church and the practice of their faith gave witness and manifestation to their loving relationship with God. Nothing separated them from their connection to God; nothing human or manmade came between them and their spiritual connection to their Maker.

You must decide for yourself how your own spiritual or religious background and beliefs or nonbelief relate to your politics and your candidacy. No matter what you believe, however, one truth is absolute: The ability to recognize the humanity in everyone allows you to see beyond clashing opinions, competing agendas, and different backgrounds. Alignment with that principle will make you a better candidate and a more compassionate, understanding, and respectful public official.

Faith to Resolution

As a leader, it's up to you to rely on your own spirituality, faith, and values as well as the facts. If you refer back to the five tenets of running for office, you'll see that Number Four is, *I will become a resource for potential resolution.* That is a noble purpose for anyone who aspires to hold public office, and it is the truest test of the leadership skills you've been working so hard to develop. It is also a critical tenet to keep in mind as you explore the relationship between faith, religion, and politics in your community and among your constituents.

It takes a lot of faith, and an unending supply of positive energy, to listen patiently to passionately opposing viewpoints. It takes fortitude to stay calm and composed when negative comments are sent your way. When religious viewpoints enter the mix, it becomes even more charged. I know, because I've been there.

My Own Spiritual Path

I was raised in the Catholic Church, although I at times found myself at odds with the institution when I held office. I also believe firmly in America as a country whose greatest resource lies with her citizens, whose beliefs and views should be respected. Our country and its political conversations are at times clumsy for that very reason—our institutions are an extension of ourselves, in all our human imperfection. That is as it should be.

During my tenure in elected office, the Catholic Church was one of the most influential institutions in my district. It had a vast and deep cultural impact, and was perhaps the largest employer in the area via its various entities.

I saw every precinct and every community as a potentially strong base for me, no matter what its party registration or religious affiliation. I was a Democrat and my district had Republican voting communities; many religious sects were present and active to some extent. I had previously defeated an incumbent Republican state senator. Republican presidential and statewide candidates did well at the ballot box in my district. I needed to pay attention and be able to express myself without partisan rhetoric, and with information, values, and ideas for solutions.

I tried to keep lines of conversation open, even when it came to deeper, more controversial subjects in neighborhoods where the Catholic Church was a strong influence and where people held more conservative views.

I wanted when I served in office to move issues forward that helped people. I discovered, though, that what "forward" looks like can be a matter of opinion. The issues at hand may have simmered below the surface for years, even generations. They might have been the cause of angry, even hateful, exchanges.

They might also link closely to a person's innermost spiritual beliefs or religious views. You might be pushing for change or a new way of thinking, only to butt up against entrenched institutions or ingrained belief systems that have a lot of momentum in the opposite direction. That momentum can be so strong it can feel as though it's dragging you backward.

Land, Money, and Religion

These types of conflicts are not simple, and it is difficult to separate facts from feelings when you face them. Those big issues often come down to a few key factors, such as land, money, and religion. These things lead nations to war. But they also can be catalysts for positive change and growth.

My faith helped me navigate these conversations and helped me to not take criticism and negative comments too personally. When people disagreed with me, I fell back on what my faith taught me. I pretended that I was the other person, and tried to understand how my decision looked to them, and why they saw it that way. Without that empathic understanding behind your explanations, you risk driving a deeper wedge between you and those on the other side of the issue, rather than drawing everyone closer to resolution.

Walking Through the Fire

Sometimes you're not going to get to a place of resolution without walking through the fire. As I have mentioned before, controversy is necessary to our society and to our political conversations if we seek positive change and accountability. If we are going to talk about subjects that are important to us, it's going to get messy. That is okay. You are dealing with people's minds, feelings, and faith. You have to move through all of it, and do so with respect, in order to get closer to the truth.

Whatever side of a controversy you stand on, know that someone stands on the other side. Recognize that God or our Source loves them, too. Mother Teresa famously referred to "Jesus Christ in all his distressing disguises." For her, that meant that she could look upon someone and see the humanity within him or her. We can all understand that concept of universal love. It is a force that favors the people on both sides of the conversation equally. By tapping into it, you can look across a minefield of disagreement at those who oppose you and treat them with respect.

You might not love what someone arguing against you has to say. But if you can find a way to respect, hear, even love the person for who they are, you have taken the first step toward having a conversation that means something. These conversations are about our core. That is why they are so uncomfortable to have. When someone threatens your core, your first instinct is to protect it.

I urge you to uncurl from that spiky, hedgehog-like ball of self-preservation, and instead subscribe to an attitude of love. You might find it quite freeing. You will be able to have more authentic conversations about issues that touch on matters of faith and religion once you see that you can still respect the other person even if they vehemently disagree with you. You will also better understand the premises beneath people's positions. You will walk away from the most heated and insulting conversations with your belief in yourself and your faith intact, and you'll keep doing good work.

The Abortion Discussion

I wrote this book to inspire you to become the best candidate possible in order to improve this country. As you run for office and serve as an elected official, you might be asked about your stance on abortion.

You might have strong personal feelings about abortion. Discussions about abortion are times when questions of religion and faith tend to surface, because for many people the two conversations are closely linked. I was asked many times to explain my stance on this issue. I'll do so again here, in the hope that reading about the process I went through will help you make your own way.

In my family, there was a sense that every baby was welcome. My father was a physician, and he believed strongly in the sanctity and uniqueness of each person, even within the womb. My pro-life position was also informed by my being Catholic, and that understanding was ratified throughout my entire young life, until high school, when some of my friends and classmates had unexpected and unwelcome pregnancies. Still, the adults and institutions in my world did not discuss the issue.

Then I went to college. As a young adult, I was exposed to many different points of view regarding abortion, and I came to realize the subject wasn't so black and white. Among my friends were people who made different decisions about pregnancy, both personally and intellectually, and it never affected my relationship with them. Much like gay marriage, I did not have much reason to wrestle with the question of whether I supported abortion rights on a personal or a political level. Most of my friends and contemporaries were pro-choice. In my own mind, I punted and did not really engage in the active pro-choice conversations. What I came to realize was that my heart and spirit could not go along with the expected and anticipated so called pro-choice stance.

When I first ran for the Legislature, there was an expectation that every female who ran for office would be pro-choice as a matter of course. But I couldn't hold that position with honesty and conviction.

As always, I let the facts lead me. I knew from my days as a practicing lawyer that if a pregnant woman was killed in an accident, there could be two lawsuits leveled against the person at fault—one for killing her, and one for killing her unborn child. That was just one of the inconsistencies that made it too hard for me to take the easy, expected position.[13]

If pinned down, I would say I was pro-life. But I knew that I wasn't pro-life the way some others were, with no caveats. I couldn't support a position that would force a woman to carry a brain-dead child to term, or to complete a pregnancy that was the result of rape, incest, or some other horror. At the same time, I wasn't in favor of abortion "on demand" throughout the entire 40 weeks of gestation.

I felt deeply that the abortion conversation was, in most cases, not informed by facts. I saw little redeeming value in the discussions surrounding the issue, on either side.

What are the rights of the mother? The father? The child? How do we factor in the latest medical and scientific advances? People's religious beliefs also came into play, and sometimes clouded their ability to examine all sides thoroughly or admit, even to themselves, that they had doubt in their minds or hearts. Although Roe v. Wade was the law of the land, it was frequently the subject of queries, and an agenda item for erosion or expansion by both the pro-life and pro-choice communities.

Getting Comfortable with an Uncomfortable Situation

At coffee hours around my community, I explained myself. It is likely the same will be asked of you as you campaign. In my district there was a clear generational split on the issue at that time. Older voters were likely to be pro-life and younger voters were likely to be pro-choice. The future was bright politically for the pro-choice community. In Massachusetts, almost every statewide official and member of Congress was pro-choice. If forced to answer what my absolute position on abortion was, I'd say "pro-life." But I also explained that we needed to have a conversation informed by ethicists, scientists, physicians, and other experts, as well as spiritual leaders. There were important questions that had no easy answer. Is gender selection a reason to end a pregnancy? Is a developmental disability a reason to terminate a pregnancy? When I finished outlining my perspective and how I got there, not too many people disagreed with me.

My feeling was, and still is, that most of us want to do the right thing for the right reason. The polarization of the non-debate on the abortion question is of benefit to no one.

The fact that those considerations weren't even present in the conversation was unacceptable to me, and I think their lack is unacceptable to most people in America as well. Yet what I seemed to find was a pro-choice community that wanted abortion on demand with no guidelines or moral and scientific boundaries, and a pro-life community that wanted every fetus protected, whatever the circumstances. I disliked the polarization and extremism these positions generated.

I looked for ways to widen the conversation so it included science, ethics, social justice, and values. I learned more about fetal development. I wanted a resolution that would stand the test of time, and I was ready to get down to the hard work of figuring it out and setting some informed and relevant guidelines.

What I experienced, though, was that because of my credentials and the fact that I was from the capital city, my not being pro-choice was disturbing to some people. I felt a lot of pressure to be accepted, and the political conversations around abortion often felt like a straitjacket I couldn't get free of.

Ultimately, I remained pro-life. Throughout my time in office, I tried to support women who had unwanted pregnancies, and to further the education and examination of the issue. I learned to be more comfortable in an uncomfortable situation, and today I am happy that I did not abandon ship. I think I chose the best of all possible paths available to me.

Leadership Is Nimble

You may find, as I did, that forces in the media or other outside influences kick up the majority of dust in the abortion discussion. Responding to what media outlets, commentators, bloggers, and others have to say publicly about abortion can lead the conversation in a direction that isn't in the best interest of you, your campaign, or the voters. It can be difficult to keep your wits about you and stay in touch with the roots of the conversation in these instances. But take heart, because no matter where you are on this issue, know that it can be done, and you can do it.

It's up to you to balance what you read and hear, and perhaps what the media puts forth about you and your fellow candidates or office holders, with what is actually in the minds and hearts of the public. When I spoke to my constituents, I found that most members of the public have a personal level of comfort or discomfort with the abortion issue and abortion policies. But they are less interested, in most cases, in a protracted, heated conversation on the matter. Most of the people in your community probably don't represent the extremes on the issue that we encounter on television, in print, and online. Instead, they make up the wide middle of the spectrum, with intensely personal, individual opinions that take many factors into account.

Most people you will encounter are not looking to have their minds changed on this issue, or to change yours. Instead, they want to know where you stand. They want to know why. Plus, they want assurance that you can withstand the heat and explain your position with clarity and conviction.

Reckless Endangerment of Children

Another issue arose during my time in the Massachusetts Legislature that brought me into direct conflict with the Catholic Church. In 2002 to 2003, it came to light that Catholic clergy had been sexually abusing children. I was Catholic, pro-life, and against the death penalty, so my positions so far had not countered those of the Church. In addition, I had enjoyed a personal and professional association with the Archdioceses, including then-Cardinal Bernard Law.

When I saw the story in the *Boston Globe* about the abuse allegations, my first thought was, "This can't be happening." But I soon realized it might be true. When the evidence became overwhelming, I called for Cardinal Law to step down. I was chair of the Criminal Justice Committee at the time, and I asked for prosecution as a matter of law in cases where evidence showed any adult had exploited children. Some in law enforcement were claiming that we did not have the proper statutes in place.

I felt sick about the victims, many of whom lived in my area. After a lot of research, I decided to file the "Reckless Endangerment of Children" bill. Its aim was to prevent any physical and/or sexual abuse of a child, and it would target all adults who were abusers.

I based the bill on the concept of reckless endangerment. If you drive a car at high speed through the park but don't hit anyone, for example, that is still considered a crime. I felt that adults who perpetrated child abuse as well as those who knew about it and covered it up should be held accountable for their conduct.

After a great deal of research from other states, especially New York, we came up with a great proposal and circulated it. On the day of the hearing, we had no one to testify in support of the bill other than me. The established groups and advocates who typically would step up for children were silent and invisible. Attorney Wendy Murphy, a non-partisan child abuse expert with a national profile, agreed to testify after outreach from my office. I co-chaired the committee hearing and left my seat to join the witness table and testify for my bill. Wendy testified. Wendy's testimony was compelling and informed the Committee and the public about the importance of our bill in protecting children from sexual assault. That was it. Then co-chair Representative Stephen Tobin and I discharged the Reckless Endangerment Bill as "ought to pass" out of the Committee on Criminal Justice.

The press hounded me. "Does this mean Cardinal Law would be prosecuted?" reporters asked me. I explained that the tragic scenario that was playing out in the church with his involvement was what gave me cause to write the legislation and that is what lawmakers are supposed to do—solve problems.

However, this public policy and conversation wasn't just about stopping the sexual abuse of children by clergy ordained in the Catholic Church—the bill would also protect a child being used as a drug mule or who was abandoned in an automobile on a hot day in a mall parking lot, or anywhere else reckless behavior was occurring. "Reckless Endangerment" could encompass many other scenarios than the one going on in the Catholic Church, and it ought to.

Although we got off to a controversial start, eventually, the Reckless Endangerment of Children bill passed on a roll call vote in both branches unanimously, and is widely used, as we had envisioned, in every district court of the Commonwealth today.[14]

The Conversations that Matter Can Be Scary

Maybe the thought of bumping up against religious institutions or even people's individual faiths intimidates you. It can be scary. You might feel like you are the only one who sees the truth. But let me assure you, yours are not the only pair of eyes that are open. Most everyone sees what you see; they may just not want to say anything. Be that voice, hold others accountable, and help people. That is where the separation of religion and faith can be a healthy move—when it allows you to focus completely on the people you serve, and remember that institutions, too, are made up of imperfect people.

These are also the times when you will bring your specific experience and expertise to bear on an important public conversation. In this instance the political and public policy assistance came from outside the established political groups and individuals. Wendy Murphy and I did not share a prior relationship. We were in fact strangers to one another. When you are a candidate it is likely that you will find allies in unexpected places. Needed change is often made possible by those on the outside with the courage and expertise to assist. In the matter of the protection of children, my legal experience, especially with some types of criminal law, and my divinity-school education prepared me to navigate the legal and religious communities. That knowledge and those experiences equipped me to lead and be useful in a profoundly difficult and troubling situation.

Your own expertise, whether it be in real estate, insurance, business, farming, education, construction, or some other pursuit, will help you along the way as well. Rely on your own knowledge, experiences, and beliefs as you make your way, and you will deepen your connection with your constituency on even sensitive topics.

There is no perfect answer in conversations that touch on religion and faith. Instead, strive to keep talking and learning in order to find common ground. Underneath the objectifying and stereotyping that dehumanizes us all, I believe God, or our Source, made us all to love and be loved.

Election Day and Beyond

*We drink from wells we did not dig, and we are warmed
by fires we did not build.*
—ANONYMOUS

Finally, all your planning, preparation, self-assessment, courage, leadership, sweat, tears, learning, and old-fashioned work bring you to the natural culmination of your campaign efforts: Election Day. It is a day to relish, and also a day to work hard. The night before, give yourself the best gift you possibly can: Go to bed early. Relax, recharge, and rest, because tomorrow you've got a long roller coaster of a day ahead.

The final standout of my campaign was the evening before Election Day, my last chance to make myself visible to the voters before they headed to the polls. There were no other special activities scheduled for the day before the election or primary, other than the general election-eve "Truman Rally."

Old-Fashioned Politics: The Truman Rally

Two different neighborhoods in the city of Boston, Dorchester and West Roxbury, hold old-time election-eve "Truman Rallies"—a local tradition inspired by presidential hopeful Harry S. Truman campaigning from the back of a flatbed truck. During these, candidates appearing on the ballot the next morning come to an open-air gathering in a local parking lot. It has all the "lights, camera, action!" appeal of a Hollywood movie set.

The Truman Rally begins just after dark, and closes after the last candidate has spoken. National, state and local candidates come out to participate in this unofficial end to the campaign season. Hundreds of people attend, and get the chance to cheer on their candidate as he or she makes a final pitch. Local opinion makers and dignitaries manage the evening and present the candidates to the hundreds of voters gathered together. The media is present as well, and the Truman Rally is often the feature-story opener for the local late-night news.

Long before I was elected, the Truman Rally was an election-eve tradition in Boston. During my tenure, Truman Rally founders began to retire from public life and, sadly, the tradition lapsed. Close friends and I decided to restore this fabled election-eve event with the special assistance of some of the original founders: Steve Slyne, Kaye Ryan, Tom Maloney, Jimmy Roberts, and others. You may want to start an election eve rally in your community or improve upon an existing rally. The rally brings the community together and improves voter participation.

With my friends the five Ws; a stellar neighborhood volunteer rally committee; financial and in-kind donations from residents, businesses, and candidates; and the great assistance of the city of Boston, our Truman Rally returned with a vengeance. The tradition continued all through my time in public service. Perhaps the most prominent and memorable aspect of our Truman Rallies was the drama of an enormous American flag proudly unfolding to drape a building more than two stories high. That flag, which served as a beautiful backdrop for the platform staging, was donated and hung by local businessman, philanthropist, Vietnam veteran, and proud American Richie Gormley.

The Harry Truman Society

ELECTION EVE RALLY

Monday, November 4, 2002

6:30 p.m.

West Roxbury, MA – At the
Municipal Parking Lot on the corner of
Centre & Hastings Streets

✯ Emcee Mr. Brian Leary, Esq., Former Channel 5 News Anchor & Current
Partner In The Law Firm of Gadsby Hannah

✯ Special Dedication Honoring The Truman Society Founders Including
Steve Slyne & Others

✯ Also, The National Anthem To Be Sung By Greg Hildreth, The Boston
Latin School Band, The Massachusetts State Police Bagpipers, The West
Roxbury High School ROTC & Other Distinguished Guests

For More Information Call Christina Hogan at (617) 722-1348 or Ken Martin at (617) 880-3218

Harry Truman rally flyer

With the exception of the rally, we reserved all our resources for a successful Election Day deployment: get-out-the-vote telephone calls, working the polls, poll checking, driving voters to the polls, etc. We even had special Election Day volunteer cards. It takes every ounce of energy and every volunteer and worker you can muster to make Election Day a success.

Please remember to vote November 7th. Polls are open from 7am - 8pm.

Marian would appreciate your assistance at the polls on Election Day. Can you help? _____

Name _____

Address _____

City/Town _____

Telephone # _____ Email _____

What time is best for you: Morning   Afternoon   Evening

After the election please join us at the West Roxbury Elks for refreshments as we watch the returns from our race and the Governor's race.

Please visit us at one of our campaign head quarters in Norwood, Dedham or West Roxbury or call us at 617-323-6333.

SENATOR Marian Walsh

Thank you so very much!!   *Integrity. Responsibility. Results.*

Election Day volunteer card

Be Your Best Candidate: Checklist ☑

Get the vote out as Election Day creeps closer:

- ☐ Learn the voter registration laws in your community, and share that knowledge.

- ☐ Offer rides to people who don't drive or who have mobility concerns.

- ☐ Get a volunteer to babysit for parents of young children who might have difficulty getting out to register or vote.

- ☐ Help voters learn the best voting method for them.

Greet the Day with Kindness in Your Heart

As you greet the day when voters head to the polls, keep kindness and generosity in your mind and heart. This is an important day, and it can play on your nerves and your heartstrings equally. Be kind to everyone, and remember the journey you took to get here. Remembering those who worked so hard on your campaign, your friends, your family, your volunteers, and everyone in the community who supported you will help you stay centered during the rollercoaster ride of Election Day, and greet it with the right measure of gratitude.

You can express your grateful heart and show your appreciation. I always gave out "Election Day" soup at every voting precinct to workers, poll checkers, and voters, opponents and supporters alike. Bobby Wiggins of Gourmet Catering, a local business pioneer and quiet patriot, provided this healthy, hearty fare. I mention Bobby because he helped me from the beginning when we held fundraisers in his small office just outside the kitchen where the food was prepared, and still is. He was just starting out, too, and is now one of the most successful and beloved caterers in New England, including at this writing for the JFK Library and Museum and the Boston Red Sox.

Alliances like these are special and sacred, because they develop around a shared sense of commitment to quality. For me, the commitment was to politics. For Bobby, it is to the best food and service possible. You will find that sense of connection and commitment with many in your community as you run for office.

For more than two decades, I continued to give out that soup on Election Day, even when my office was not on the ballot. It became more than an offer of nourishment, transforming into an expression of gratitude and commitment to everyone who toiled hard to make the electoral process work.

Get Out and Be Seen

What is the first item on your Election Day agenda? Vote. Get to the polling place early and be one of the first in line to exercise this all-important American privilege and duty. After you've cast your vote, choose where and how you will make the most of the day. Your goal on Election Day is no different than any other day of your campaign: visibility and connection.

Election Day laws dictate how close you can be to the voters at polling places. Follow the Election Day voting regulations relative to political activity that you secured earlier in your campaign. Remember, Election Day is about the voter. You want to avoid dust-ups with election officials at the polls or local news stories depicting your campaign violating the Election Day voting laws. Long before Election Day arrives, you should have scoped out your district and your neighborhood for your Election Day position.

There are plenty of places in your community where voter traffic will be high on Primary Day or Election Day, and where you can park, be personally visible all day long, and stay in compliance with the voting regulations. Ask yourself, *Where can I meet the most people who may vote on this day? How can I make contact with them?* Find a spot where you can get close enough to voters to be seen, recognized, and noticed, and where you can express your gratitude for their engagement and consideration.

Election Day is your time to smile, shine, and put forth all the positive energy you gathered during your time campaigning. If you've been following along with the steps in this book, you're certainly not a new face at this point. The voters have seen you every day, everywhere. Today, they will recognize your face again and be reminded that you are present, willing to work, and the right person for the job.

I stayed close to polling areas all day on Election Day, with short breaks for food and to sit down. My goal was to shake hands with, smile at, and make eye contact with as many people as possible throughout the day.

Pace yourself. This day is about you and the voter. Resist the urge to drive around town on Election Day or chat with friends and neighbors while voters slip by. These pursuits are not the best use of your time. Your mission is to make contact with as many voters as possible. Avoid engaging with your opponents or becoming drawn into what they are doing or saying. When a supporter takes up too much of your time, gently remind them that you know they want you to greet other voters too, because that is the way you will all succeed. And of course, thank them.

Every Primary Day and Election Day, I remained at the polling location and campaigned, voter by voter, until the polls closed at 8:00 p.m., and then a volunteer drove me home to receive the early results from our poll checkers and get ready to join everyone at the election night gathering.

I stood at the most dense urban voting precinct in the Roslindale section of Boston, at the Saint Nectarious Greek Church in Roslindale Square.[15] Candidates and volunteers stood shoulder to shoulder. At this voting location, modern-day patriots worked for their candidate or ballot question with passion, expectation, and commitment. It was a keen competition, and it was inspiring to witness.

Dealing with Distractions

You may find yourself quietly receiving an incoming stream of information throughout Election Day from your poll checkers/counters. Sometimes your volunteers may pass you pieces of paper that describe the voter turnout and trends. What do you do with these tiny missives? Slip them in your pocket and wait to review them at a time when a voter does not need your attention.

Avoid having discussions with volunteers or other workers while you are out meeting and greeting the voters at the polls. If a problem is brought to your attention that requires your immediate judgment to resolve, have it passed to you in writing. Then discreetly write down your recommended solution and pass it back. Resist getting on your cell phone to start receiving or sending texts, or to engage in lengthy discussions. These activities will distract you from the day's most important mission: engaging the voter. Plus, you could be overheard or seen as people walk by you, and the voters will perceive you as disengaged or distracted. That's exactly what you do not want, today of all days.

Don't let your fellow candidates become a distraction, either. It is likely that your rivals and their supporters are in the same location you are on Election

Day, some or all of the time. Recognize that they have the same right to be there. If feasible, move to some other favorable location rather than dilute your effectiveness with your rivals, especially if they are there first.

Remember, when it comes to Election Day visibility, the early bird catches the worm. Be the first to claim the best spots. There is an unofficial rule that the first candidate to arrive "owns" the spot, and others move along to another.

However, those unspoken rules don't always prevent negative interactions from occurring. I experienced a situation where a rival abandoned his town, and arrived at my home voting precinct late on Election Day, where I was greeting voters, and attempted to draw me into conversation. Opponents' workers have also stood near me and spoke loudly and negatively about me within earshot of voters as they entered the building to vote.

In situations like these, remember above all the kind and loving heart that brought you to this place. Reside there mentally and emotionally, and smile—no matter what. Surround yourself with people who support you. On Election Day, end every day during my campaigns, people were with me. They helped buffer and defuse the occasionally unwelcome behavior of others.

Absent this behavior, it is preferable to view your rival as a positive expression of America's political process. See them as someone who enriches and broadens the conversation, just as you do. Fly above the clouds. Today is the day to celebrate that process and stay in contact with the desires and hopes that called you and your rivals alike to run and try to serve. That's all that matters.

What Is a Poll Checker?

Helping people vote ensures a successful election. The most valuable resources you have at your disposal to help you reach out to voters on Election Day are your volunteers. Among those Election Day volunteers are people who help out at the polls to keep track of who voted. These are commonly called "poll checkers," although they may be called by another name in your home state.

You need to get authorization from your municipality or county, but you are allowed to station poll checkers at voting areas. These volunteers sit in a chair beside the voting authorities and check off people's names from your list (remember your "good lists"?) as they leave.

Since you've been maintaining and updating those lists throughout your campaign with information gleaned from door-knocking, events, and phone-bank calling, you know who is likely to vote for you. Today, of all days, you want to make sure they show up. You also can size up the voter turnout, and judge if a lot of people who aren't "your people" are arriving to cast a vote. If that is the case, you've got a real race on your hands, and will need to ensure all of your supporters get to the polls.

Poll checkers check off people as they vote. That information is picked up by other volunteers from the voting places, and then delivered to the campaign headquarters. There, other volunteers will compare the poll checkers' lists to your list of who you think your supporters are, to determine whether or not your supporters have voted. Don't underestimate the value of this old-fashioned approach. As of this writing, I have been involved with campaigns on the national level that attempted poll checking electronically and which experienced crashes, due in part to high Internet demand on Election Day causing electronic freezing and other failures. These problems may have been solved by the time you read this section, but it is always wise to have a back-up plan for electronic systems, and to be prepared to resort to the tried-and-true paper and pencil if necessary.

If you find gaps in the list—supporters who have not yet voted—it's time to mobilize. This is a job for your Election Day volunteers. They must call, email, or visit anyone who hasn't voted to make sure they intend to vote and determine if they need help getting to the polls. The connection between the information your poll checkers collect and your Election Day phone bank volunteers is an important one.

The people your phone bank volunteers are checking on are your "Number 1s," the people you ascertained as likely to vote for you. The phone bank will call them to ask if they voted today, find out if they need a ride to the polls, or to offer any other assistance to help them cast their vote. These calls serve as good reminders, and also can bring in a few more votes in your favor. They can be a deciding factor in a tight race. The lists provided by your poll checkers will help the phone banks reach out to the right people who can make a difference with their votes.

Many states also allow early voting. Find out if yours does, and begin the poll-checking process as soon as voters are eligible to vote. Your goal is to get your supporters to vote as early as possible. Poll checking helps facilitate that process.

As the Polls Close

At the end of the voting day, when the polls close, the warden will announce the votes. Your last poll checker should be there to write down the results. There might be a wait if the office you are running for is far down on the ballot, because the ballot results are usually announced in order.

Once the poll checker has the results, he or she should call them in to campaign headquarters, or wherever you designate. You may choose a text or an email. My preference was telephone for privacy and accuracy. A slip of the finger may lead to an incorrect report via text or email. I received the results at home via telephone from my campaign headquarters.

Encourage supporters not involved in the collection or publishing of voting results to go to the election-night hall, where you can post results on big boards as they come in. That way, everyone will be involved, and will know as soon as possible exactly what is happening. In addition, this helps keep your headquarters as calm and organized as possible as the final poll checkers drop off the written count from their precinct assignment.

This is the time to assess how many votes you received, what your rivals received, and perhaps take stock of other races as well. I always had the poll counter call in the count then bring the actual piece of paper with the vote tallies on it to campaign headquarters. All this was done efficiently and with utmost privacy. Double check everything, get the counts in writing, and sign off on them before any results are announced to your supporters. You want absolute accountability in this process, and you don't want to create confusion or disseminate bad information.

Here are two samples of how election results look when tabulated. The first is for the primary when I ran for the state Senate, and the second is for the general election.

City/Town	M. Walsh	M. Casey	S. Teehan	All Others
Boston	8,962	5,915	971	0
Dedham	3,363	1,600	886	0
Medfield	342	308	299	0
Walpole	1,137	748	687	0
Westwood	1,055	724	434	0
Totals	**14,859**	**9,295**	**3,277**	**0**

Election results for 1992 state Senate primary

City/Town	M. Walsh	C. Lane	All Others	Blank Votes
Boston	21,241	9,551	1	2,504
Dedham	6,729	6,104	1	632
Medfield	2,086	4,045	0	221
Walpole	4,451	6,433	1	640
Westwood	3,327	4,475	0	593
Totals	**37,834**	**30,608**	**3**	**4,590**

Election results for 1992 state Senate general election

Walsh bests five opponents to win primary

By Ed Griffin
Staff Writer

PARKWAY -- Powered by a well-organized campaign, first-time candidate Marian Walsh emerged from a field of six Thursday to clinch the Democratic nomination in the race for the 10th Suffolk legislative seat.

Walsh, a virtual unknown in the area until seven months ago, garnered 29 percent of the vote and topped the ticket in ten of the sixteen precincts to pull ahead of the other candidates in the race.

Walsh was followed in the primary by Gregory Haugh, Kathleen Ryan, George Hailer, Edward Englert and John Miller.

"It's good to know a grass roots campaign can still win," said Walsh. "When I decided to run, I found a lot of people who believed in me, came to the campaign and brought a lot of friendship. We came up with a tremendous pool of talent. A very dedicated, nice family has come together."

Walsh said she did not try to gain the support of any particular neighborhoods or voting groups, but instead, distributed campaign efforts evenly across the district.

Walsh finished first in ten of the 16 precincts in the race. She showed particular strength in the Hancock Woods, Billings Field, Bellevue Hill and Stratford-Clement neighborhoods. She also attracted a strong percentage of votes in the neighborhood located between Holy Name Church and the VFW Parkway.

Walsh will face Independent Kenneth Phalan, a local lawyer, in the November general election. Two years ago, Phalan won 49 percent of the vote in his bid to unseat incumbent Charles Doyle. Phalan is active in youth basketball, St. Theresa's Parish activities. He is a Boston College graduate and a Marine Corps

WALSH -- See page 8

10th Suffolk District

The following are the vote totals in the Democratic primary for the 10th Suffolk state representative seat.

ENGLERT	660
HAILER	868
HAUGH	1997
MILLER	395
RYAN	1244
WALSH	2189

Local paper reports state Rep primary results

Riding the Election Night Roller Coaster

Within an hour of the polls closing, you'll probably have a pretty accurate picture of where you stand. You'll know which precincts act as barometers for how the election is likely to fall. You are aware of the areas where you are strong, and those where your opponent is stronger. You know all that information by this time because of your exhaustive research and work during the campaign.

It can be a roller coaster of a night after the polls close. Precinct by precinct, the official results come in. Most likely, your supporters are waiting in a restaurant or function room you've arranged as your post-election meeting spot. They might be eating good food, socializing, and anxiously awaiting results. Anything can happen, so be ready for the unexpected. Stay centered, calm, and kind. Above all, don't expend a lot of energy by celebrating or despairing too early. In my first election, I lost the first four precincts that reported. I was sure I had lost the election. Then I proceeded to win the next sixteen. Pace yourself!

Arrive at your election-night venue to wholeheartedly thank your supporters and volunteers. When you win, it's time to celebrate. But hold off on giving your acceptance speech or talking to the press until your rivals have conceded, if possible. I do remember two instances when campaign opponents did not concede. After a respectful length of time, I gave my acceptance speech.

Your most important task tonight is to thank everyone who helped you get to this point, and acknowledge the many contributions of time, energy, spirit, and money that drove your campaign forward. Also, be sure to acknowledge the great engagement of your worthy opponents and their supporters, and express the hopefulness that you will earn their support and consideration in the future.

The morning after Election Day, I staged a thank-you standout at Holy Name Rotary, the place where so many voters from my district had seen my smiling face over the many months I campaigned. I had thank-you signs made, and we displayed them proudly.

The Real Work Begins

Your first Election Day is behind you. Now the real work begins. The fifth and final tenet from the start of this book alludes to what lies ahead: *You will work hard for positive change.* When you started down this road, you decided to feed your hunger for positive change by working for it and running for office. Way back then, you took the first step with the simple act of deciding to run.

You might not realize it, but you make an impact every day you are out campaigning, and it is a mark that will endure beyond any decisions you might make as a public official. By proving that everyday people from all walks of life can get out there and run, you have shown others just like you what is possible and what they themselves could achieve if they only try. By digging deep to uncover your own untapped leadership potential, you could bring forth a whole line of new, undiscovered leaders who were just waiting for someone to be the first to jump in the pool. That is the kind of positive change that leads to progress.

Every time you stand up for what you believe, speak out for truth, research the facts, and engage in public discourse during your campaign, you ripple the waters. Those ripples keep expanding outward with their own momentum, and reach into every corner of your community.

A New Beginning

I am a lucky person. I am an American and the recipient of a legacy, one that I did not build, but that was born of the creative and courageous leadership of others. Those who have come before us conceptualized and grew a community of people. We call that community America.

Above all, this book is about that potential. It is meant to encourage you to seize it and manifest it. I also hope it teaches you how to do those things, and shows you that it is not all that hard. What I've presented here is just a framework. It's up to you to make it work for your time, place, interests, and personality. I encourage you to use it as a springboard for your own participation and accomplishments, and to make it your own.

But one thing that is certain is that greater involvement in politics by a greater cross-section of the American people can only bring about improvement, progress, and positive change. Connect deeply to that positive and inspired place within yourself, and you will see America at her best as you run for office and win.

· · ·

Appendix: **Speeches**

THIS IS THE SPEECH IN SUPPORT OF GAY CIVIL MARRIAGE I GAVE AT THE MASSACHUSETTS CONSTITUTIONAL CONVENTION IN 2004.

People do not want to change the Constitution.

People do not want gay marriage.

We give witness to our Constitution every day but perhaps no more expressly than when we, the elected representatives of the people, meet in the Constitutional Convention for the Commonwealth of Massachusetts. The purpose of our Constitution is beautifully stated in the preamble: "To furnish the individuals (who compose it) with the power of enjoying in safety and tranquility their natural rights and the blessings of life."

The essence of the Constitution is described in the preamble as well, by explaining that we as citizens are "entering into an original, explicit, and solemn compact with each other; and of forming a new Constitution of civil government, for ourselves and posterity."

Which constitutional right, which you now enjoy, do you want to give up?

The freedom from unreasonable searches and seizures?

Or the right to trial by jury?

Or the right to free speech?

Or the right to assemble peaceably, as we do today inside and outside of the statehouse?

Why do we wish to take away the constitutional right to marry from some of our constituents?

Do we wish to take it away because some established institutions demand that of us?

Why do these institutions make such demands upon us?

Why?

Perhaps we should read again our compact with one another—our Massachusetts Constitution—and remember that it is Article II of this Constitution that protects and respects the freedom of religion, the right and duty of worship, public worship and religious teachers and the separation of church and state.

Constitutional rights run to individuals, not to groups or organizations or institutions.

So today I ask:

> What Constitutional rights would individuals participating in religious activities like to give up?

> Would individuals who worship surrender their own religion, and enjoy a state religion?

> Would individuals who are clergy like to give up the authority to perform civil marriage ceremonies that this legislature gave them in 1692?

In Article I, when we discuss "Equality of People and Natural Rights," we see that, "All people are born free and equal and have certain natural, essential and unalienable rights among which may be reckoned the right of enjoying and defending their lives and liberties; that of acquiring, possessing and protecting property; in fine, that of seeking and obtaining their safety and happiness. (Equality under the law shall not be denied or abridged because sex, race, color, creed or national origin. 1976.)"

Throughout this document there are references to happiness, and the pursuit thereof. It doesn't say that "all people are born free and equal and have certain natural, essential and unalienable rights, except gays and lesbians."

Do we want to make that change? Do we want our compact with one another to say that some of us are not equal? Because of Article II in our Constitution, no religion, church, or sect will be expected or required to marry gay couples.

What about the word "marriage" scares us when we discuss gay couples?

Why will we give so many benefits in the proposed amendments, but expressly place in our Constitution a ban on gay marriage?

We realize, from earlier testimony at this convention, that marriage as an institution has had a very colorful history. It has not been historically one man and one woman. It has been one man and many women. Women were property. Marriage was often about land and inheritance rights.

It has already been well treated, at earlier meetings of this convention, that marriage is perhaps healthier today than it has ever been in the history of the institution. Perhaps this is so, based on the fact that people today now marry for love and happiness.

The SJC did not amend our Constitution. They interpreted our Constitution. That is their function. They did not hijack democracy, or diminish the legislature or dismiss the citizenry. They heard a case before them and applied the law.

What the SJC did do, in this legislator's view, is stunning—their decision is ahead of our mainstream culture, ahead of my own sensibilities. I cannot say that I am comfortable—but I can say that our compact, our Constitution, is working, is working hard and is alive and well—applying in our culture, with our knowledge and our moral development, the principles of equality and happiness.

My level of comfort is not the appropriate monitor for the constitutional rights of my constituents.

For many of us, if everything was the same—seven couples sued, the case was heard—and the decision came down on the opposite side, there would be few complaints about the process, about the court, or about the public having the right to vote.

Perhaps what is really going on is not our objection to the process but our dislike for the outcome. Perhaps we just don't like the decision. Perhaps we are just too uncomfortable with the "marriage" word.

Well, it is well established in testimony, at this convention, and in Article II of our Constitution, that no religion is required to marry gay couples. It's also established that in Massachusetts and in the U.S. Constitution, religions have no right to marry anyone. A church's authority to perform civil marriage is derivative from civil government, and this civil government allowed clergy to perform civil marriage ceremonies via statue in 1692. Before the legislature gave this authority, clergy provided pastoral and ceremonial functions and had no civil authority to marry anyone.

Gay Americans die for our country, adopt children, and we are silent. Yet we find our voice to take away their constitutional right to marry.

The level of comfort with civil unions seems to be growing rapidly— but not marriage, even though marriage is a civil union.

But we all know how important words and symbols can be.

In prior debates at this convention we have heard that "the people have the right to vote. Let the people vote." No matter how often this is stated, it doesn't make it true.

As a matter of constitutional history, the people have addressed this very point. The people decided at the ballot box on November 5, 1918, the very process that we are exercising today—the people decided that they wanted the legislature to vote not once but twice and then the matter may come to the ballot for the citizen's review. On November 5, 1918, American women did not have the constitutional right to vote.

This process, to take away a citizen's constitutional right, requires that we as elected representatives vote at two consecutive Constitutional Conventions. The process does not direct the legislators to vote yes—the Constitution requires us to make a judgment to vote "yes" or "no."

A legislator who feels it is in the best interest to protect this constitutional right, and who does not wish to amend the Constitution, would vote "no."

We traveled this road before.

In his opening address to the delegates of the 1918 Massachusetts Constitutional Convention, Governor McCall made the following comments: "The mere counting of people does not establish what is right and what is wrong, for justice in every case cannot rest upon the will of the more numerous any more than upon the will of the stronger. The few who are at the moment stronger have no right to trample upon the many, and on the other hand, the many who by the power of numbers in democracy are stronger, have no right to oppress the few."

The public has supported this very process to avoid mob rule and avoid foolish outcomes.

The same threats to family, marriage and even natural law were proclaimed when we as a nation wrestled with:

- The voting rights of women

- The property rights of women and minorities

- Equal protection of the disabled and mentally ill

- Credit protection and educational opportunities for women and poor people

- Interracial marriage

- An integrated military.

This is where we work it out—here in Massachusetts, here in the Bay State—where we advance the human condition, navigate and perfect our understanding of being human and pursuing happiness.

For we know that our compact with one another, our Constitution, is not abstract or remote. Rather, our compact is contemporary and realized daily in each of our lives.

We are evolving and growing in our knowledge and understanding of our humanity. From little things to big—we are moving like a moral glacier to a better place. At one time we cleaned our teeth with sugar. We saw dementia and epilepsy and diabetes as manifestations of Satan and God's displeasure.

We are learning more and more about our brain, our genetics, our chromosomes, and our chemistry.

This knowledge in tandem with our compact with one another—that we are created equal and hold equal claim to pursue happiness—is the American Dream, the nature and essence of America.

We have always moved the course of humanity forward, because of our hope, because of our faith. We recognize and acknowledge the truth of our own dignity and humanity and that of one another.

The truth in Massachusetts is now shining more brightly. Our citizens who are gay can now claim more fully their equality among us. And we, we are good enough and strong enough to assist in our fellow Americans' equality, and in their pursuit of happiness.

Where else in the course of human history, where else on this planet, can this progress be made, if not in Massachusetts?

I thank my constituents for the honor and privilege to represent them and to participate in this convention. It is perhaps one of the most important and significant experiences of my life. I am grateful.

I recognize the disappointment and the criticism that my decision has received. I am sensitive to, and aware of, the difficulty that this has presented to many of my relationships—my family, my friends, my supporters, and my constituents.

An open mind, an informed conscience, and an honest deliberation of what is right, and true, and just for my constituents and for the commonwealth is my concern.

We as legislators have the right to take this right away. We can decide to change the court's action—take this right away—or we can allow this right to stand. It is my hope that we affirm the Constitution and the rights it affords, because the gay individual is owed the promise and hope of America fully and equally that is our compact, our Constitution. The compact with one another, the Constitution, has always required us individually to reach beyond our moral emotional grasp. Then we actually begin to become the nation that we want to be. It is not always easy or quick to be true to our destiny but it is my duty to try, and try I will, because,

> "All people are free and equal and have certain natural, essential, and unalienable rights; among which may be reckoned the right of enjoying and defending their lives and liberties; that of acquiring, possessing and protecting property; in fine, that of seeking and obtaining their safety and happiness. Equality under the law shall not be denied or abridged because of sex, race, color or national creed."

• • •

THIS IS A SPEECH GIVEN TO ANNOUNCE MY PLAN TO RUN FOR RE-ELECTION TO THE MASSACHUSETTS STATE SENATE.

Thank you for allowing me the opportunity to serve you and for all of the personal and professional enrichment you have brought to my life. In my eyes all my constituents are equal and equally important. Whether or not I know you, whether or not you are a donor, or a citizen, or even a voter, born or unborn, you are important to me.

Whether you are un-enrolled, a Democrat, or a Republican, I am here to be helpful and give you an equal voice in the promise and hope of America.

I ask you tonight for your vote and a chance to serve you again, in the next legislative session of the Massachusetts state Senate.

Thank you very much.

• • •

THIS IS A MEMORIAL DAY OBSERVANCE SPEECH FROM 2008.

As President Harry Truman proclaimed, "They have earned our undying gratitude," so today we show that our gratitude is not dying—but very much alive, by our physical presence, here this Memorial Day morning, 2008.

We come together to do, what this day was created for: to remember. That is our charge, our active, open, and public remembrance that our fellow Americans have died for us to live.

Thank you to all who prepared the cemeteries, placed the flags, and organized this ceremony. Thank you to my colleagues in government who give meaningful service to our country and community. Today we recognize also our friend and fellow patriot Richard Gormley.

For 142 years, grateful Americans have come together in ceremony to remember these brave people. We remember and acknowledge their bravery in good times and in bad. We remember their sacrifice whether the war is popular or has little support.

This act of service that for some in our military involves one's death—usually while still healthy and young, with promise and great expectation for their own personal future.

Their dream is personal to them, their loved ones and a grateful nation.

We need to know about their stories. We need to share them, and then their valor will live forever through each of us.

Allow me briefly to give you just one example of an ordinary serviceman whose actions were honored in a White House ceremony just weeks ago.

Petty Officer Second Class Michael A. Monsoor, a Navy SEAL, age 25, was awarded the Congressional Medal of Honor for his bravery beyond the call of duty in action in Iraq. His mortal sacrifice saved the lives of two fellow Navy SEALs and several Iraqi soldiers. This award is presented only after an Act of Congress, and it rewards and remembers acts of gallantry in combat "far and above the call of duty."

The fallen SEAL's parents, George and Sally Monsoor, accepted the Medal of Honor on their son's behalf during a ceremony marked with full military tradition by a grateful nation.

Michael Monsoor was a machine gunner providing security at a sniper lookout post on September 29, 2006, in Iraq.

A fragmented grenade thrown by the enemy hit his chest and bounced to the floor; Monsoor was positioned next to the only exit from the rooftop position and could have escaped harm easily.

Instead he threw himself onto the grenade. Monsoor used his body to shield the others from the blast, saving two nearby SEALs and eight Iraqi soldiers.

Monsoor expired a half hour later. Monsoor became the first SEAL to receive the Congressional Medal of Honor for actions in Iraq and the second to receive the award since September 11, 2001.

He joined 3,445 other recipients who have received the ultimate award for heroism in the face of grave danger.

Young Michael Monsoor was a child with asthma and overcame great odds to successfully complete the rigorous training to become a U.S. Navy SEAL.

This is something for us to remember, to know about and talk about. Michael Monsoor was an individual who did not let us down—he was not selfish or small. He was not even expected or required to fall on that grenade, and if he had chosen to escape he would not have been criticized. This love, this courage he was taught and he became. Let us remember Michael Monsoor and how we have benefited and prospered by the love and courage of so many.

God guide and bless America, let us show "our undying gratitude" to those who have died for us with love and courage. Have a grateful and blessed Memorial Day.

• • •

Endnotes

1 Ansolabehere, Stephen, "Run for Office", Boston Review, May/June 2011, http://www.bostonreview.net/BR36.3/stephen_ansolabehere_run_for_office.php

2 The office of the Secretary of State of Massachusetts has a terrific website for this type of information, http://ma.electionstats.com. I'm sure most every state has a similar site.

3 Volunteer card and bumper sticker produced in collaboration with KHJ, Brand Activation, Boston, Massachusetts.

4 Secretary of the Commonwealth Elections Division, 1989; Public Document No. 43 Massachusetts Elections Statistics 1988, Commonwealth of Massachusetts.

5 Ellen O'Brien, "Body of Jeffrey Curley is Found In Maine River In Court, Prosecution Details Cambridge Boy's Final Hours," Boston Globe, Oct. 8, 1997, at A1.

6 Adrian Walker and Sue Wong, No death penalty, by one vote Momentum for a state law is halted as House member changes his mind, Boston Globe, Nov. 7, 1997 at A1; Journal of the House, Tuesday October 28, 1997, Roll Call No. 138, Commonwealth of Massachusetts (1997); Journal of the House, Tuesday November 6, 1997, Roll Call No. 154, Commonwealth of Massachusetts (1997).

7 Chapter 119 of the Acts of 1995, "An Act Making Appropriations for the Fiscal Year Nineteen Hundred and Ninety-Five to Provide for Supplementing Certain Existing Appropriations and For Certain Other Activities and Projects, Mass Acts and Resolves, 1995; Sue Wong, "Weld Backs Hancock Woods Preservation," Boston Globe, Aug. 19, 1995, at A1.

8 Beverly Schwartz, Massachusetts Constitutional Convention Roll Calls on Same-Sex Marriage Amendments, http://www.ir.bbn.com/~bschwart/marriage/rollcall.html; Journal of the House, Wednesday, February 11, 2004, http://www.mass.gov/legis/journal/hj021104.pdf; Journal of the House, Thursday, February 12, 2004, http://www.mass.gov/legis/journal/hj021204.pdf; Journal of the House, Thursday, March 11, 2004, http://www.mass.gov/legis/journal/hj021204.pdf; Journal of the House, Monday, March 29, 2004, http://www.mass.gov/legis/journal/hj032904js.pdf

9   William Galvin, 11/02/2004 State Election, p.6 http://www.sec.state.ma.us/ele/
    eleres/stateeleres04.pdf; William Galvin, Return of Votes for Massachusetts State
    Election, November 7, 2006, p. 14 http://www.sec.state.ma.us/ele/elepdf/rov06.pdf

10 Higginbotham, Evelyn, "In Politics to Stay: Black Women Leaders and Party Politics
    in the 1920s," Unequal Sisters: An Inclusive Reader in U.S. Women's History, Vicki L.
    Ruiz with Ellen Carol DuBois, New York and London, Routledge, 2000, pp 289-300.

11 Chapter 140 of the Acts of 2003, Section 26, An Act Making Appropriations for
    Fiscal Year 2004 to Provide for Supplementing Certain Existing Appropriations
    for Certain Other Activities and Projects, http://www.malegislature.gov/Laws/
    SessionLaws/Acts/2003/Chapter140; Chapter 139 of the Acts of 2009, 4510-0600,
    An Act Making Appropriations For the Fiscal Year 2007 for the Maintenance of
    the Departments, Boards, Commissions, Institutions and Certain Activities of
    the Commonwealth, for Interest, Sinking Fund and Serial Bond Requirements
    and for Certain Permanent Improvements, http://www.malegislature.gov/Laws/
    SessionLaws/Acts/2006/Chapter 139

12 Chapter 28 of the Acts of 2005, An Act Providing for Capital Repairs to the Jim
    Roche Memorial Rink in the West Roxbury Section of the City of Boston, http://
    www.malegislature.gov/Laws/SessionLaws/Acts/2005/Chapter28; Uncorrected
    Proof of the Journal of the Senate, May 31, 2005, http://www.mass.gov/legis/
    journal/sj053105.htm

13 Massachusetts Supreme Judicial Court, Abortion Decision, 2013, http://boston.
    com/metrodesk/2013/05/21/sjc-upholds-murder-convictions-two-men-who-shot-
    and-killed-unborn-baby-orange-line-train/ZyTPg1SWO6JpgyFglfvxDN/story.html

14 Uncorrected Proof of the Journal of the Senate, June 19, 2002, http://www.
    mass.gov/legis/journal/sj061902.htm; Chapter 322 of the Acts of 2002, An Act
    Establishing the Crime of Reckless Endangerment to Children, http://www.
    malegislature.gov/Laws/SessionLaws/Acts/2002/Chapter 322; Mass. Gen. Laws ch.
    265, § 13L (2012).

15 City of Boston Resident List, Ward 20, Precinct 14 pp. 9833-9836 (2011)

About the Author

State Senator Marian Walsh has never lost an election. Beginning with her first run for the Massachusetts House of Representatives in 1988 as a political unknown, Walsh was re-elected to a second term then went on to serve nine consecutive terms in the Massachusetts State Senate until 2011. She was the first woman to hold her House and Senate seats and also held ranking positions, including Majority Whip. She was nominated for the prestigious John F. Kennedy Profile in Courage Award, honoring those in public service "who, acting in accord with their conscience, risk their careers by pursing a larger vision." A former chief administrative officer for the Suffolk County District Attorney's Office, Walsh is also an attorney. She was graduated from the Newton College of the Sacred Heart, Suffolk University Law School and Harvard Divinity School. Currently a public affairs consultant and leadership coach as well as a lecturer of ethics and leadership at Northeastern University, Walsh resides in Massachusetts with her husband, Paul V. Buckley.